CHANNEL CROSSINGS
CROSSINGS
AROUND BRITAIN

Peter Cumberlidge

CHANNEL CROSSINGS
CROSSINGS
AROUND BRITAIN

for Power and Sail

ADLARD COLES
8 Grafton Street, London W1

Adlard Coles
William Collins Sons & Co. Ltd
8 Grafton Street, London W1X 3LA

First published in Great Britain by
Adlard Coles 1990

British Library Cataloguing in Publication Data
Cumberlidge, Peter
  Channel crossings
  1. English Channel. Pilots' guides
  I. Title
  623.89′22336

ISBN 0-229-11852-6

Typeset by Ace Filmsetting Ltd, Frome, Somerset
Printed and bound in Great Britain by
Mackays of Chatham plc, Chatham, Kent

CONTENTS

ACKNOWLEDGEMENTS

Some of the contents of this book first appeared as a series of articles in *Practical Boat Owner* and I am grateful to George Taylor, *PBO*'s Editor, for his suggestions and comments when the series was being written. My thanks also to Des Sleightholme for his advice on passage-making in the North Sea; to Jane Sandland, for drawing the originals for most of the charts and for combing the text for errors; to Joyce Cumberlidge and James Briggs, for their help with detailed proof-checking; and to the various crews who have sailed aboard *Stormalong* over the years and helped us to arrive safely, sometimes in spite of the decision-making.

INTRODUCTION

Most cruising skippers spend many enjoyable hours each season planning, discussing and wondering about passage-making. Where to head for, what about the weather, how do the tides influence departure and arrival times, what about alternative ports-of-call if the weather turns foul, what happens if fog closes in? Sometimes this quite complex decision-making can mean more stress than fun at the time, although the magical satisfaction of arriving usually makes up for all the tensions in the end. Often, when you are trying to interpret a dodgy forecast, speculate about the progress of fronts and depressions, or visualise likely sea conditions, it can be helpful to talk to others in the same predicament. But this can also be confusing, because you rarely find two skippers faced with the same circumstances – they will have different types of boat, different crews, varied levels of experience, and perhaps completely different timetables and reasons for going cruising in the first place.

The aim of *Channel Crossings* is to help skippers make prudent decisions about specific passages. The book stems from my own cruising experiences, but has drawn upon numerous deliberations and discussions with other navigators on occasions when I or they have been trying to work out a plan,

calculate the best time to catch a tide, or make the most of a dismal shipping forecast. I hope that relatively inexperienced skippers might benefit from mulling over some of the pros and cons of different courses of action, and that seasoned skippers might also be interested in the discussion of passages they may know well, even though they might not always agree over the question of strategy. Some of the crossings have appeared as individual articles in *Practical Boat Owner*, and I am grateful to George Taylor, *PBO*'s Editor, for his suggestions and comments when those features were first written.

The book's title is not intended to suggest a preoccupation with English Channel passages. On the contrary, I hope it will evoke that feeling of anticipation which most yachtsmen feel when faced with a crossing of any open stretch of water. Although I cover many of the popular passages across the English Channel, I have also included a crossing of the southern part of the North Sea, a passage across Biscay, a passage from Falmouth to the inimitable south-west coast of Ireland, as well as crossings of St George's Channel, the Irish Sea and the North Channel.

I have tried to make the discussions applicable to both sailing and motor boats. Although the times and speeds in the main body of each chapter relate to passages under sail, there is a section for each crossing which deals with factors relevant to fast motor boats. I have also included a special chapter on high-speed navigation. Passage-making at 15 or 20 knots has its own particular problems. Careful planning is vital and it's important to use electronics and instruments to full advantage.

A summary of important lights and radio beacons is given at the end of each chapter. Although such details are prone to slip slowly out of date, I nevertheless decided that it would be more useful to include this information than to leave it out. You will no doubt be navigating with a current almanac and reasonably up-to-date charts, so any changes to lights, buoys or beacons can usually be verified fairly easily. On the other hand, I did make a conscious decision not to specify passage waypoints too precisely. Although many navigators now use Decca, Loran or Sat-nav and are therefore accustomed to planning their passages in terms of legs between waypoints, I thought it would be a mistake to draw up a detailed compendium of waypoints accurately worked out to several decimal places of latitude and longitude.

When all discussions are done, it is always the skipper's responsibility to decide how much to hold up to windward or stay up-tide, how far to clear a particular danger, whether to pass east or west of this or that sandbank, or which route to follow when making a landfall. So where I have suggested a useful waypoint, I have deliberately not given a latitude and longitude which might run the risk of being entered straight into a Decca sailplan without careful consideration. After all, one of the great rewards of passage-making comes from trusting our own judgements and getting there ourselves. I rather hope that we never reach the stage of keying-in routes from a passage directory and selecting 'auto-nav mode'.

Peter Cumberlidge
Llanfair Kilgeddin, 1990

1 HARWICH TO FLUSHING

Boat owners based on the Essex and Suffolk coasts look naturally towards the Netherlands as a versatile and rewarding cruising ground, although a passage across the S part of the North Sea from Harwich to Flushing can often be more daunting than, say, a crossing from the West Country to Brittany at the Atlantic end of the English Channel. Numerous offshore banks fringe the coasts for many miles on both sides of the passage and you can expect heavy shipping in the middle and in the approaches to Zeebrugge and the Westerschelde. Although there are plenty of buoys well off the Belgian and Dutch coasts, the landfall shore is low and featureless and difficult to identify by day in hazy visibility.

Many of the banks on the Continental side may be crossed safely in moderate conditions, but heavy weather can cause dangerous breakers over the shallowest areas. It then becomes important to wend your way between the banks, and yet the rather uncertain tidal streams in their vicinity conspire to make the navigator's job more complicated. The streams tend to run more quickly over the shoals or be accelerated between them, and these local effects depend considerably on the actual state of the tide at the time. The flood in this part of the North Sea runs broadly SW at maximum rates of about 2½–3 knots, but both the stream and the height of tide can sometimes be affected by heavy weather up in the N or by sustained westerly gales.

Although I have called this chapter 'Harwich to Flushing', it is useful to consider the passage from Harwich to Ostend in parallel. These two trips have much in common and most navigators crossing this corner of the North Sea will probably keep both possible destinations in mind. You can reckon on 75–80 miles from Harwich entrance to Ostend, depending on how much bank-hopping you can manage off the Belgian coast. Harwich to Flushing is more like 95 miles, with the last leg involving something of a dog's-leg into the Westerschelde. Neither passage strategy is overly affected by tidal considerations out in open water, but you need to catch the flood into the Westerschelde if you are bound for Flushing. Neaps are preferable to springs if you have a choice, because you are less vulnerable to nasty wind-over-tide conditions near the banks if the wind should freshen.

Different skippers have their own views about the best times for setting off, negotiating shipping lanes and making landfalls. Other things being equal, I

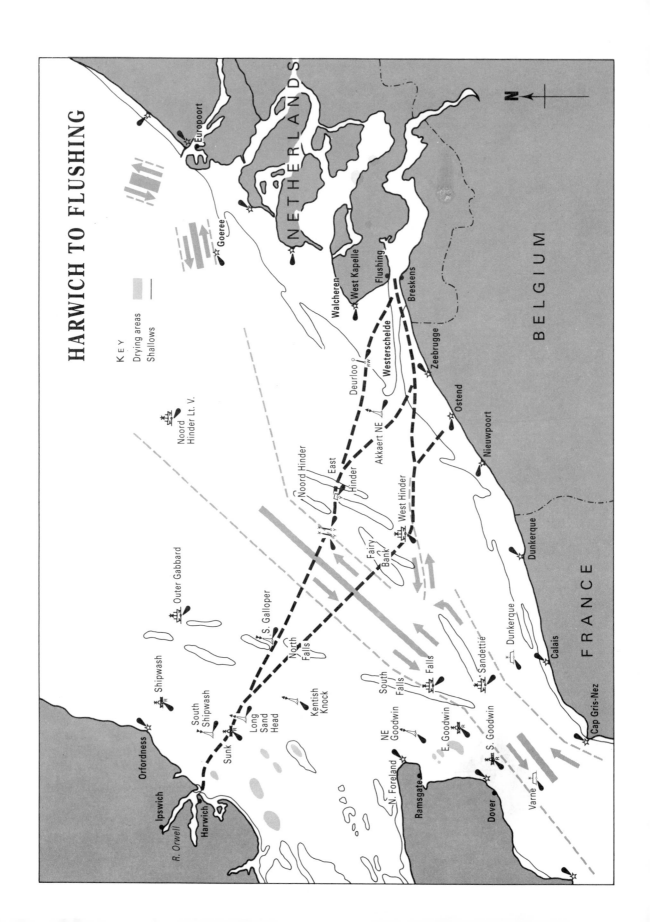

have always had a preference for setting off on a longish passage in the late morning. You will have had a long sleep the night before, enjoyed a leisurely breakfast, and had plenty of time to get ready for sea, buy any last-minute stores, and so on. By setting off near the middle of the day, most of the crew should be at their best, and you will have the afternoon to settle down on board before the evening meal and the start of the watch-keeping routine.

Much depends, though, on what kind of speed you expect to make. The passage from Harwich to Ostend might take anything between 12 and 17 hours if you were to average between 4½ and 6 knots under sail, so you have the option in high summer of setting off at dawn or just before dawn and aiming to arrive in daylight. Many crews would prefer this to a night passage, although if the wind turns light or contrary and your average speed is much less than planned, you will find yourself approaching the coastal banks and making your landfall just as darkness is coming on.

For the long passage to Flushing, there is something to be said for a late afternoon start. If, for example, you were to clear Harwich entrance at something like 1600, an average speed of 4½ to 6 knots would put you off the outer approaches to the Westerschelde between about 0400 and 0800 the following morning. This can fit in well with the tides off the Belgian and Dutch coast because, ideally, you'd want to pick up the first of the E-going stream to carry you into the Westerschelde. This starts running 1 hour or so before HW Dover, and a dead neap high water at Dover normally falls somewhere between about 0530 and 0800 BST. The disadvantage of this schedule is that it takes you through the main shipping lanes at night—no great problem in clear conditions, but not much fun if visibility is poor.

Leaving Harwich

Harwich harbour, of course, gives access to the various marinas and numerous moorings on the River Orwell up to Ipswich, as well as the less populated upper reaches of the River Stour. The Orwell and the Stour are both attractive stretches of water and the newest marina—Shotley Point—lies at their confluence just opposite Harwich town. Shotley Point Marina is the nearest to the harbour entrance and is a convenient point of departure for a passage to Ostend or Flushing.

Traffic is the main hazard as you leave or arrive at Harwich, with ferries and container ships coming and going from Parkeston Quay and Felixstowe. The deep-water channel leads S past Landguard Point and then a little N of E out to Harwich fairway buoy, but yachts following this general route should keep just *outside* the buoyed channel to the W and S as far as Cork Sand red buoy. An alternative, although much shallower, way out for yachts is via the Medusa Channel, which leads more or less due S from Landguard N-cardinal buoy, down past Pye End fairway buoy, close W of Stone Banks red can buoy, and then out to the Medusa green conical buoy. Strangers usually find the main channel more straightforward. Having reached Cork Sand buoy, you need to work SE for about 7 miles, past Roughs Tower and its buoys, and then make a position somewhere between South Shipwash S-cardinal buoy and the Sunk light-float.

On Passage

To Ostend: If you are definitely bound for Ostend, your track from just E of the Sunk light-float will be about 132°T for 42 miles to the West Hinder light-vessel. This line takes you ½ mile E of Long Sand Head N-cardinal buoy, about 4 miles (depending

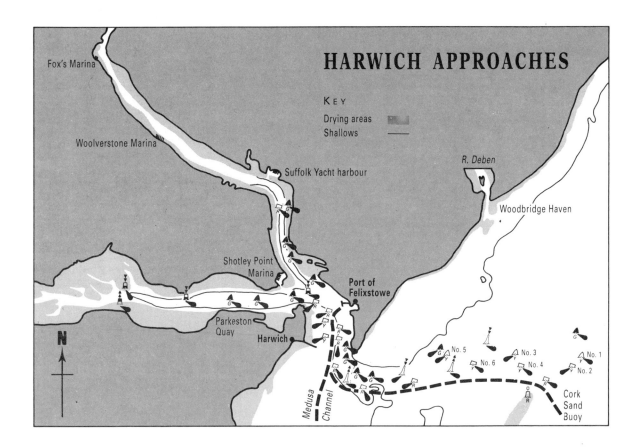

HARWICH APPROACHES

KEY
Drying areas
Shallows

Fox's Marina

Woolverstone Marina

R. Deben

Suffolk Yacht harbour

Woodbridge Haven

Shotley Point Marina

Port of Felixstowe

Parkeston Quay

Harwich

Medusa Channel

No. 5
No. 3
No. 1
No. 6
No. 4
No. 2

Cork Sand Buoy

N

on the tide) SW of the South Galloper S-cardinal buoy and then across the narrow North Falls bank. The 10-mile-wide band of shipping lanes lies between North Falls and the West Hinder, but your track cuts across the traffic almost exactly at right angles.

From the West Hinder light-vessel, the coastal approach lanes lead eastwards for about 10 miles to the Kwintebank N-cardinal whistle buoy, which then lies 10 miles NW of Ostend. The traffic can be busy along this stretch and it's best to cross the lanes (only two miles wide) at right angles from the West Hinder, and then keep just *the wrong side* of Oost-Dyck green whistle buoy and *A-Zuid* green conical buoy before turning SE towards Ostend.

In quiet or moderate weather, and if you have definitely decided to make for Ostend, you can take a short cut across the banks, rather than go right out to the Kwintebank buoy. From the West Hinder light-vessel, cross the lanes at right angles to a position midway between Berguesbank N-cardinal buoy and the Oost-Dyck green buoy. From here make good ESE for 10 miles to the Middelkerkebank buoy and then SE across the Oostendebank to Ostend, about another 8 miles.

To Flushing: If you are heading for Flushing, however, there are some possible variations to your strategy which depend largely upon the weather, tide and sea conditions likely to be prevailing as you approach the Westerschelde. The coastal banks

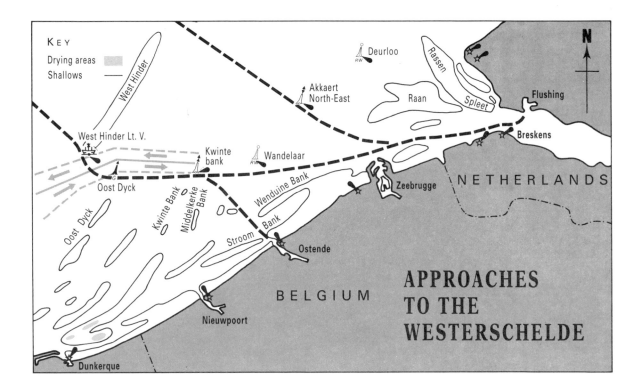

KEY
Drying areas
Shallows

West Hinder

Deurloo
RW

Rassen

Akkaert
North-East

Raan

Spleet

Flushing

West Hinder Lt. V.

Kwinte
bank

Wandelaar
RW

Breskens

Oost Dyck

Kwinte Bank

Middelkerke Bank

Wenduine Bank

Zeebrugge

N E T H E R L A N D S

Oost Dyck

Stroom Bank

Ostende

B E L G I U M

**APPROACHES
TO THE
WESTERSCHELDE**

Nieuwpoort

Dunkerque

between Ostend and Flushing are nothing like as shallow and intricate as they are further W, between Calais and Ostend, say, but you still have to make a careful landfall, especially with an onshore wind. One plan is to proceed as though you were bound for Ostend, picking up the West Hinder coastal approach lanes, crossing to the S side, and following E just *outside* the buoyed fairway as far as the Kwintebank N-cardinal buoy. From here you have the options of turning off for Ostend, a little over 10 miles to the SE, or, if the tide serves, continuing E to join the long buoyed Wielingen channel which leads close N of Zeebrugge into the Westerschelde.

In reasonable weather, and provided the visibility looks as if it will be satisfactory, yachts of modest draught can aim to approach the Kwintebank N-cardinal buoy directly, by passing over the S part of

the West Hinder Bank. From the Kwintebank buoy you have the choice of carrying straight on for Ostend, or turning left for the Westerschelde.

The coast between Ostend and Zeebrugge is comparatively straightforward to approach from seaward, and in normal weather it is safe to set an offshore waypoint anywhere between the Kwintebank buoy, which lies 10 miles NW of Ostend, and the Akkaert North-East E-cardinal buoy, which lies a similar distance NW of Zeebrugge. The only proviso is that you ought to avoid the shallowest part of the West Hinder Bank, a 3-mile tongue with less than 4 m over it in parts, just over 16 miles WNW of the Akkaert North-East buoy.

This piece of navigation is fairly easy if you are equipped with Decca, but you will otherwise have to locate the yellow routing buoys that the ferries use on their crossings to and from Zeebrugge. In this case, your passage will probably consist of a series of distinct legs, the first being from Sunk light-float to the South Galloper buoy, about 16 miles at 116°T. From the South Galloper, you can then aim to make good 117°T for just under 20 miles to find a pair of yellow buoys moored close together right on the SE edge of the up-channel shipping lanes. This track crosses the lanes almost at right angles and the two buoys are moored about 6 miles NW of the shallowest part of the West Hinder bank.

There is another yellow routing buoy moored a mile or so NE of the northern tip of this shoal patch, not quite 7 miles at 100°T from the first pair. If you set a course to pass close N of this buoy, you are then clear to make for the Akkaert North-East E-cardinal buoy, 15½ miles at 114°T, and thence SE to join the Scheur or Wielingen Channels into the Westerschelde.

In quiet weather you can aim to enter the Westerschelde via the Deurloo Channel, a relatively shallow but direct route which cuts SE into the estuary close E of the area of shoal water known as the Raan. For this you have to find Deurloo fairway buoy, moored just over 8 miles NE of Akkaert North-East, and then follow the lateral buoys SE towards Flushing.

The trouble with the Deurloo when you are coming straight across from England is that it may be difficult, at the start of your passage, to predict the sea conditions, visibility and state of tide with which you may be faced when arriving off the Westerschelde. In a freshening north-westerly, say, it would be safer to use the Wielingen Channel and make your approach much farther W than the Deurloo buoy. In poor visibility, too, it is easier to come in somewhere between Kwintebank N-cardinal buoy and Akkaert North-East. There is an eastern channel into the Westerschelde, the Oostgat, but you would normally only use this on a passage from Harwich if, for example, fresh south-westerly weather had set you much further E than planned.

Heavy Weather on Passage

This S corner of the North Sea is decidedly bleak in heavy weather. The relatively shallow soundings make for short steep seas and most of the banks seethe with breakers, especially in a weather-going tide. Finding a port of refuge is not easy on either side of the passage from Harwich to Ostend or Flushing, and often the safest bet will be to stay at sea rather than feel your way through a maze of off-shore shoals towards a harbour whose narrow entrance may itself be a maelstrom of turbid water. The low coasts of Belgium and Holland are tricky to identify in clear visibility, let alone in driving rain and spray, and the menace of shipping adds yet another unpleasant factor to the mix.

One should not set off from Harwich, therefore, without having carefully considered all the implications of the forecast, and worked out strategies for coping with both likely and unforeseen shifts in the weather. In some respects, a traditional south-westerly summer gale is the least malevolent fate that can befall a well-found yacht, because there is at least plenty of sea-room out to the NE. If you do decide to heave-to, though, you have to take account of the eventual veer and the likelihood of a significant period of strong north-westerlies—a dangerous wind if you are too near the Dutch or Belgian coasts.

Provided that the wind on a warm front backs no farther than SW and doesn't become too savage, most yachts should still be able to lay a close-reefed course for the West Hinder light-ship (allowing generously for leeway) in the hope of reaching Ostend via the coastal approach lane and Kwintebank N-cardinal buoy. The timing of the cold front, however, can again be critical. As long as the heavy weather stays from the SW, you do begin to get some lee from the French coast and its offshore banks as you draw inside the West Hinder. But a sudden veer to the NW and a few hours of near gale-force winds from that direction can catch you in just the wrong position, within 12 miles of the Belgian coast with Ostend and its outer cordon of shoals now transformed into a dangerous lee shore.

It is worth keeping Zeebrugge in mind as a possible bolt-hole, its huge sheltering breakwaters lying about 18 miles E and a little S from the Kwintebank buoy. The large outer harbour is safe to enter in most weathers and the approaches are comparatively uncluttered by banks. There is a comfortable berth for yachts in the Visserhaven, reached by turning to starboard behind the inner W pier and then heading SSW towards the entrance to the Brugge canal. Zeebrugge would usually be a safer entrance than Ostend if you had reached the West Hinder coastal approach lanes and a cold front veer had left you with a stiff north-westerly to contend with.

The estuary of the Westerschelde is not a friendly place for a yacht in heavy weather, especially in an onshore wind against an ebb tide. However, the West Hinder coastal approach lanes and the Wielingen Channel constitute a major shipping fairway, deep (for these parts) and well-buoyed. It is normally safe to enter the Westerschelde by this route as long as the wind allows you to sail more or less E and you are snugged down and prepared for steep seas. E of Zeebrugge, the Raan bank provides a certain amount of shelter from onshore swell, and much of the real weight will have gone from the seas by the time you reach Flushing or Breskens.

The important tasks are to keep careful track of your position and avoid shipping, for which the best plan is to stay just the wrong side of the buoys on the S side of the fairway.

Heavy weather from the E or NE can be a grim prospect on this North Sea crossing. A strong easterly makes it almost impossible to lay a course for Ostend, while the Belgian and French coasts farther W have much shallower and more dangerous banks in their approaches. The only consolation with an easterly, if you do manage to hold up to windward, is that you should obtain some shelter from the land as you draw inshore. A north-easterly has a long fetch and puts a nasty selection of dangers under your lee: the numerous shoals of the Thames Estuary, the Goodwin Sands, the congested Dover Strait shipping lanes and the maze of offshore banks between the West Hinder and Calais. A strong north-easterly has almost no redeeming features and, if you are ever in doubt about whether or not to sail, you will be wise to stay tucked up in Harwich harbour, perhaps exploring the many agreeable watering holes of the River Orwell.

Ramsgate is a possibility if you need to run off before a north-easterly, although it is well over 30 miles to leeward of the direct track between Harwich and the West Hinder. The important point about approaching Ramsgate from the NE is that you should aim to make your landfall well over towards the North Foreland rather than risk getting too close to the NE Goodwin buoy. North Foreland RDF beacon (*301.1kHz, 'NF', 50M, cont.*) or its VHF beacon (*Ch. 88, 'ND', 20M, alt with Calais*) are useful aids for this purpose.

Since its considerable extension, Ramsgate harbour is easier and safer to enter in heavy weather than it used to be, although it is important to follow the buoyed channel which leads in from due E. A useful Decca waypoint for yachts coming down from the Foreland is a position directly between Ramsgate No. 3 green conical buoy and No. 4 red can.

If you meet any kind of heavy weather on the passage from Harwich to Flushing or Ostend, you may, given enough warning, decide to turn back for Harwich rather than risk becoming embroiled among the banks and shoals off the Dutch or Belgian coasts. But care is also needed for this tactic, especially in poor visibility, since you need to follow a safe track between the Shipwash bank, which lurks to the N of the Harwich approach, and the various shoals to the S—Kentish Knock, Long Sand Head and, as you near the entrance, Cork Sand. The Sunk light-float RDF beacon is useful as you are making this approach, despite its limited range (*312.6kHz, 'UK', 10M, cont.*).

Poor Visibility

Coping with shipping is the worst aspect of mist or fog on this passage. The main lanes are busy enough, but there are also the Ostend and Zeebrugge ferries to contend with. As you make your landfall, you meet ships entering or leaving the Westerschelde, or anchored at one of the waiting areas in the approaches.

Although Decca can obviously take some of the edginess out of the navigation, there are plenty of buoys, aids and other clues for those, like myself, who still prefer to find their way about the seas using simple low-tech methods. Coming out from Harwich in poor visibility, it is not difficult to follow the S side of the deep-water channel to Cork Sand red can buoy and then set a course to skirt Roughs Tower and its buoys. Once you are past the Roughs, you can home down to the Sunk light-float by RDF and take your departure from there.

There are no RDF beacons in the Westerschelde estuary, so without Decca it is not prudent to con-

template a direct approach from seaward, either via the Akkaert North-East E-cardinal buoy or the Deurloo Channel. If, therefore, it looks like being murky all the way across, there is much to be said for making for the West Hinder light-vessel, whether you are eventually bound for Flushing or Ostend. West Hinder RDF beacon only has a 20-mile range (*305.7kHz, 'WH', 20M, No. 3*) but is quite adequate for homing purposes once you get close. Having reached the light-vessel, if the sea is calm the easiest route to Ostend is to cross the coastal approach lanes and find the Oost-Dyck green buoy, which has a whistle. From here set a course to make good 115°T for 16½ miles, keeping Ostend main lighthouse RDF beacon (*305.7kHz, 'OE', 30M, No. 4*) on this bearing. This track leads straight to Ostend pierheads, passing E of the Middelkerke-bank buoy, across the Oostendebank, just over ¼ mile NE of the Stroom N-cardinal whistle buoy and not quite ½ mile NE of the Stroom E-cardinal buoy. The soundings over the banks will give you a fair idea of your progress.

Having reached the West Hinder light-vessel, you can decide to buoy-hop into the Westerschelde if the tide serves, keeping just outside the shipping fairway to the S. This is not too difficult even in quite poor visibility, so long as you don't panic if you miss one of the buoys. There is a certain amount of cross-tide until you get into the estuary and then the streams broadly follow your track. The low-range RDF beacon on Zeebrugge breakwater (*296.5kHz, 'ZB', 5M, Nos. 1, 2*) is useful when entering the harbour or passing by on your way into the Westerschelde.

Once E of Zeebrugge, it is safe to edge close inshore on the echo-sounder if visibility is very poor and you prefer to stay well clear of the shipping channel. You then have the option of following the S shore of the estuary round to Breskens, which will probably be preferable to crossing the fairway and trying to find the entrance to Flushing.

High-speed Factors

Skippers of fast motor boats contemplating a passage from Harwich to Flushing need to be specially diligent about planning all the likely legs before setting off. There will be little opportunity or time when under way to worry about working out new routes and courses between the various offshore banks, which may become more or less negotiable as sea conditions change. There will also be plenty of shipping to keep both helmsman and lookouts occupied.

Unless you know this sea area and its coasts well, it makes sense to keep to the main routes between principal navigation marks, rather than wondering whether this or that short cut would be feasible. Having left Harwich by keeping just W and S of the deep-water channel as far as Cork Sand red buoy, you might take your departure from a position ½ mile NE of the Roughs Tower. From here, the passage plan could lead to the approaches to Ostend first and be built round the following principal waypoints:

1—Midway between Sunk light-float and Shipwash S-cardinal buoy
2—¼ mile SW of South Galloper S-cardinal buoy
3—¼ mile W of the West Hinder light-vessel
4—¼ mile S of Oost Dyke green buoy
5—¼ mile S of Kwintebank N-cardinal buoy
6—Ostend pierheads
For the Westerschelde:
7—¼ mile due S of Wandelaar fairway buoy
8—1 mile NW of Zeebrugge W breakwater head
9—1 mile NW of Nieuwe Sluis lighthouse
10—¼ mile SE of Flushing's Buitenhaven W mole head

There are, of course, numerous buoys to follow once you reach the West Hinder light-vessel, particularly in the approaches to the Westerschelde E of Kwintebank N-cardinal buoy.

Radar is helpful when you are coping with the main shipping lanes during the middle part of this passage, but it can almost be more of a hindrance once you reach the outer approaches to Ostend and the Westerschelde. You may then find it difficult to distinguish between ships and buoys, or to differentiate between various buoys in the same vicinity. From any distance offshore, the low coasts of Belgium and Holland practically sink into the sea as far as most small-boat radars are concerned.

There are three useful Racon beacons on the English side of this passage: Harwich Channel No. 1 buoy (*'T', 10M*), Sunk light-float (*'T', 10M*), and South Galloper light-buoy (*'T', 10M*). The West Hinder light-vessel provides a positive target, although it will seem like any other ship until you discover it is not moving.

Pilot Books, etc.

Admiralty NP28, *The Dover Strait Pilot.*

North Sea Passage Pilot, B. Navin, 1st edn 1987, published by Imray Laurie Norie and Wilson.

North Sea Harbours: Calais to Den Helder, J. Coote, 6th edn 1988, published by Barnacle Marine.

Adlard Coles Pilot Pack, Vol. 1, B. Goulder, 1st edn 1989, published by Adlard Coles.

The East Coast, D. Bowskill, 2nd edn 1987, published by Imray Laurie Norie and Wilson.

East Coast Rivers, J. Coote, 13th edn 1988, published by Yachting Monthly.

The Cruising Association Handbook, 7th edn 1990, published by the Cruising Association.

Admiralty Charts

No. 1406—Dover and Calais to Orfordness and Scheveningen

No. 1183—Thames Estuary

No. 2052—Orfordness to The Naze

No. 1872—Dunkerque to Flushing

No. 125—Approaches to Ostend

No. 325—Westerschelde, Ostend to Westkapelle including Flushing

Tidal Atlases

Admiralty NP249, *Thames Estuary.*

Admiralty NP251, *North Sea, southern portion.*

Dutch Hydrographic Office, *Stroomatlas Westerschelde.*

Tidal Streams (times based on HW Dover)

Position	W-going stream starts	E-going stream starts
Off Cork Sand buoy	−0530	+0100
South Galloper S-cardinal buoy	−0530	+0100
West Hinder light-vessel	+0600	HW
Off Ostend	+0445	−0045
1 mile N of Zeebrugge breakwater	+0440	−0140
Westerschelde, Nieuwe Sluis	+0315	−0300

Tidal Differences and Heights

Place	Time of HW on Dover	MHWS	MLWS	MHWN	MLWN
		Heights above chart datum in metres			
Harwich	+0045	4.0	0.4	3.4	1.1
Ipswich	+0105	4.2	–	3.4	–
Ramsgate	+0020	4.9	0.4	3.8	1.2
Ostend	+0115	5.0	0.2	4.1	1.1
Zeebrugge	+0125	4.8	0.3	3.9	1.1
Breskens	+0210	4.8	0.4	3.9	1.0
Flushing	+0210	4.8	0.4	3.9	1.0

Important Lights

English coast:

Orfordness (*Fl, 5s, 24M; FRG, 14M, 15M*); Harwich
fairway buoy (*Iso, 5s, RWVS, whis*); Sunk light-float (*Fl2,
20s, 24M*); Outer Gabbard light-vessel (*Fl4, 20s, 24M*);
South Galloper buoy (*Q6+LFl, 15s, whis*); North Foreland
(*Fl5, WR, 20s, 21M, 18M; R vis 150°–200°, W
elsewhere*)

Belgian coast:

West Hinder light-vessel (*Fl4, 30s, 24M; Fog-horn Morse
'U', 30s*); Nieuwpoort main light (*Fl2R, 14s, 21M*);
Ostend main light (*Fl3, 10s, 27M*); Blankenberge main
light (*Oc2, 8s, 20M*); Zeebrugge, Heist mole head (*OcWR,
15s, 20M, 18M; W 068°–145°T, R 145°–212°T, W
212°–296°T; fog-horn 3+1 90s*).

Westerschelde:

Kruishoofd (*IsoWRG, 8s, 8M, 5M, 4M; R 074°–091°T,
W 091°–100°T, G 100°–118°T, W 118°–153°T, R
153°–179°T, W 179°–198°T, G 198°–205°T, W 205°–
074°T*); Nieuwe Sluis (*OcWRG, 10s, 14M, 11M, 10M; R
055°–084°T, W 084°–091°T, G 091°–132°T, W 132°–
238°T, G 238°–244°T, W 244°–258°T, G 258°–264°T,
R 264°–292°T, W 292°–055°T*); Flushing, Buitenhaven
west mole head (*FR+IsoWRG, 4s, 5M; W 072°–021°T,
G 021°–042° T, W 042°–056°T, R 056°–072°T*);
Koopmanshaven main light (*IsoWRG, 3s, 12M, 9M, 8M;
R 253°–270°, W 270°–059°T, G 059°–071°T, W
071°–077°T, R 077°–101°T, G 101°–110°T, W 110°–
114°T*); Westkapelle (*Fl, 3s, 28M*); Noorderhoofd
(*OcWRG, 10s, 13M, 10M; R 353°–008°T, G 008°–
029°T, W 029°–169°T*).

RDF Beacons

English coast:

Sunk light-float (*312.6, 'UK', 10M, cont.*); Outer Gabbard
light-vessel (*287.3, 'GA', 50M, No. 4*); Noord Hinder
light-vessel (*287.3, 'NR', 50M, No. 6*); North Foreland
(*301.1, 'NF', 50M, cont.*); North Foreland VHF beacon
(*Ch. 88, 'ND', 20M, alt with Calais*); Falls light-vessel
(*305.7, 'FS', 50M, No. 1*).

Belgian coast:

West Hinder light-vessel (*305.7, 'WH', 20M, No. 3*);
Ostend main lighthouse (*305.7, 'OE', 30M, No. 4*);
Zeebrugge breakwater (*296.5, 'ZB', 5M, Nos. 1, 2*).

Weather Forecasts (all times GMT except where otherwise stated)

BBC shipping forecast areas:

Thames, Dover

VHF coast radio stations:

Orfordness—0803, 2003, on Ch. 62
Thames—0803, 2003, on Ch. 02
North Foreland—0803, 2003, on Ch. 26
Scheveningen—0930, 1530, 2130, on Chs 26 and 83
Ostend—0648, 0820, 1720, 1848, on Ch. 27
Dunkerque—0633, 1133, on Ch. 61

Marinecall:

Tel. 0898 500 455/456

Local radio coastal forecasts:

ILR Ipswich (Radio Orwell)—at local times 0600, 0800,
1200, 1600, 0000. Frequencies: *1170 kHz, 257 m,
and 97.1 MHz FM*

Met Office forecasts:

London Weather Centre, Tel. 01 430 5627

2 DOVER TO CALAIS

Mention the English Channel crossing from Dover to Calais and you conjure up a kaleidoscope of popular images—white cliffs, day trips to France, salt-caked smoke stacks. To many non-sailors, a ferry crossing of the Dover Strait is the epitome of sea travel to foreign parts. To yachtsmen, even the apparently mundane aspects of this passage are invariably tinged with a sense of history and romance. For you cannot set off from Dover pierheads without feeling some kinship with all those seafarers down the ages who have made the same departure under sail alone. Time was when a packet-boat could have taken 12 hours to beat across to Calais against a stiff south-easterly—worth a thought as you are slicing along at some undreamt-of angle to the apparent wind.

These days, of course, the Strait is one of the busiest seaways in the world, with shipping movements monitored by the Channel Navigation Information Service run by Dover Coastguard and the French 'Crossma' station at Cap Gris-Nez. Negotiating the traffic separation scheme is now the most daunting aspect of a passage between Dover and Calais. Not only do you have to face a procession of fast-moving ships, there is also a requirement to cross the lanes at right angles, regardless of what the tide happens to be doing. *The Dover Strait Pilot* notes that: 'Low powered vessels and sailing vessels should . . . not make allowance for the tidal stream while crossing, if by so doing they will not have a heading nearly at right-angles to the traffic flow.'

Your enforced strategy, therefore, will be one of dashing across the 10-mile band of lanes as quickly as possible while keeping careful track of where the tide is taking you. Because of the powerful streams in the Dover Strait—up to 3½–4 knots at top of springs—it is best to time your departure so that the overall effect of the tide works in your favour. Since Calais is not exactly opposite Dover, but about 8 miles farther up-Channel, you would prefer to experience a net set to the E, if it could be arranged. At the same time, were you to leave Dover while the tide is SW-going, you wouldn't want to be carried too close to the Varne LANBY and its narrow shoal.

The shortest distance from Dover across the Strait is effectively about 17 miles, to the edge of the shallows that lie to the NE of Cap Gris-Nez. This line, something between 135° and 140°T, leads across the shipping lanes more or less at right angles. At an average speed of 4½–5 knots, you would cover this distance in approximately 3½–4

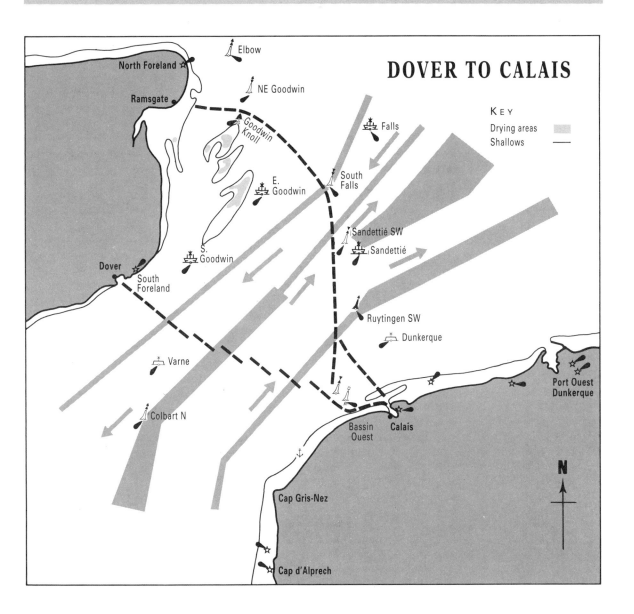

DOVER TO CALAIS

KEY
Drying areas
Shallows

Elbow

North Foreland

NE Goodwin

Ramsgate

Goodwin Knoll

Falls

E. Goodwin

South Falls

Dover

S. Goodwin

Sandettié SW

Sandettié

South Foreland

Ruytingen SW

Dunkerque

Varne

Port Ouest Dunkerque

Colbart N

Bassin Ouest

Calais

N

Cap Gris-Nez

Cap d'Alprech

hours. If, in that time, you were to experience 6 miles of north-easterly set, you should end up somewhere near the outer end of the Calais approach channel, about 1 mile to the W of CA6 red buoy. From this fairway position, it is only about 3½ miles due E to Calais pierheads, preferably with the up-Channel stream still in your favour. Beware of cross-set as you come into Calais harbour, because the tide is free to flow between the pier piles at anything up to 4 knots.

Setting off

Near neaps, you can carry a fair tide by leaving Dover west entrance at HW Dover. You should then experience about 4–5 miles of north-easterly set in the next 3½ hours, depending on weather conditions. At springs, with much faster rates, it is better to leave 2 hours before HW Dover; the tide will be more or less slack for the first hour and you'd be less likely to be sluiced too far E. This earlier departure time is no problem when leaving from the outer anchorage, which most yachts on passage would probably be doing if the weather was fair. If you are coming out of Wellington Dock, though, you are constrained by the earliest locking-out time, normally 1½ hours or so before HW near springs.

One drawback with these strategies is that you end up with a longish wait in Calais harbour before being able to lock into the Bassin Ouest and the Port de Plaisance. If you reckon on 5 hours for the passage, and even if you manage to get away 2 hours before HW Dover, you will be arriving at Calais 3 hours after HW Dover, which is 2½ hours after HW Calais. The dock gates open from about 1½–2 hours before to ½–1 hour after local HW, so you will have at least 8 hours outside in the Avant Port. This can be uncomfortable, but there are always plenty of comings and goings to watch in the harbour. You can either lie alongside the northern half of the quay which immediately faces the Bassin Ouest, just below the harbour office, or else use one of the mooring buoys.

It is equally important to pay close attention to timing on the return passage from Calais to Dover, although, if you work the tides to best advantage, you will be faced with several hours' wait in the Avant Port before starting the passage. A good time to set off is about 5 hours after HW Calais (5½ hours after HW Dover) at neaps, and 3½ hours after HW Calais (4 hours after HW Dover) at springs. The same reasoning applies. At neaps, the set provided by the middle 3½–4 hours of the SW-going stream will carry you nicely down-Channel opposite Dover if you take your departure 1 mile or so W of CA6 red buoy and set off on a course at right angles to the shipping lanes, something like 315°T. At springs, it is usually better to start a bit earlier, while the tide is still slack or weakly NE-going, otherwise you can end up with more south-westerly set than you need. Much depends upon the average speed you expect to make good.

Traffic and Port Controls

The traffic in and out of Dover can be formidable to visitors, especially if you are accustomed to small harbours or quiet river moorings. The flow of ferries, jetfoils and hovercraft often seems to be continuous, the latter making a particularly devilish noise. Hovercraft use the W entrance to Dover harbour, which yachts should also use except in an emergency. The E entrance is reserved for the ferries.

Both entrances have a control tower and set of traffic signal lights which should be obeyed religiously. The signals apply to all vessels, including yachts, as follows:

—Three fixed red vertical lights against you mean that you should not proceed.
—Green-white-green vertical lights mean that you may proceed only when you have specific orders to do so.
—A quick flashing white is a warning light, which means that you must keep clear of the entrance that you are approaching.

For instructions on VHF, call Dover Port Control on Ch. 74. If you don't have 74, call on Ch. 16 and prepare to switch to Ch. 12.

When crossing the shipping lanes, there is normally no need for yachts to make contact with the Channel Navigation Information Service, but you should listen on Ch. 16 or dual-watch 16/11 and be ready to switch to Ch. 11 for navigational warnings or weather forecasts.

At Calais harbour, full international port traffic signals are shown from the control tower at the Gare Maritime, but yachts should not react to these signals. Look out instead for three white vertical lights which give priority to small vessels. Calais port control can be contacted directly on Ch. 12, before entry if possible. This channel is also used to contact the Écluse Carnot if you are bound inland for the Canal de Calais.

Ramsgate to Calais

Since its ambitious extension in the late 1980s, Ramsgate has become an increasingly important port, with the development of commercial facilities in the new outer harbour making more space available for yachts in the Royal and inner harbours. The entrance is now much easier and safer in heavy weather, and the inner marina is a sheltered and attractive place to lie.

At about 32 miles, the passage from Ramsgate to Calais is longer than the Dover trip and complicated by having to circumvent the Goodwin Sands. You can pass inside or outside the Goodwins, although the outside route usually allows you to make best use of the tide. If you leave Ramsgate entrance about 4 hours after HW Dover, you will have 1 hour of slack water to reach Goodwin Knoll green conical buoy, which lies 4 miles due E true from Ramsgate outer pierheads. Keep just outside

the Ramsgate dredged approach channel on this leg, either to the N or the S.

From Goodwin Knoll, the next leg is SE for just over 9 miles, allowing for the SSW-going stream so as to pass close S of South Falls S-cardinal buoy at springs and 1 mile or so SW of it at neaps. From the South Falls, set a course to the S for Calais CA4 W-cardinal buoy, allowing for the strengthening SW-going stream so as to pass 1 mile W of Sandettié SW W-cardinal buoy, 1½ miles W of Ruytingen SW green buoy, and close W of RCW N-cardinal buoy.

From the CA4 buoy, it is less than 4 miles along the shipping channel to Calais pierheads. You can take a short cut over Ridens de la Rade bank so long as the sea is quiet and you are within a couple of hours of local HW. For the return passage to Ramsgate, the ideal time to leave Calais is about 2 hours before HW Dover, in order to carry a full period of NE and N-going tide. However, the earliest you can leave the Port de Plaisance is usually 1½ hours before HW Calais, which is about an hour before HW Dover. The NE stream will be well under way by the time you have cleared the entrance, so you need to average a good speed to avoid picking up a foul tide before you get to Goodwin Knoll.

Heavy Weather on Passage

The Dover Strait is not a pleasant stretch of water in heavy weather. A strong wind over a spring tide kicks up a nasty steep sea which, as well as being grim in its own right, will also make avoiding shipping that much more difficult. One consolation is that a south-westerly or north-easterly will be a reaching wind between Dover and Calais, although between Ramsgate and Calais these winds will only be free in one direction. You might think that because the Dover–Calais passage is quite short there would be no real excuse for being caught out in heavy weather, but in fact the proximity of the two ports tends to mean that yachtsmen waiting to cross are more inclined to 'give it a go' in the belief that the unpleasantness shouldn't last too long.

One obvious danger if you are coming back from Calais in a strong south-westerly is having the Goodwin Sands not very far under your lee as you approach the English coast, probably with the tide just about to turn NE-going. This would make you very vulnerable to any gear failure on the last part of the crossing, which could itself be more likely in the steep wind-over-tide seas you would be experiencing. Think twice, therefore, about making a dash back from Calais if conditions are dubious. If you are pressed for time, there is always the option of leaving your boat in the Port de Plaisance and coming back on a ferry. If you are not in a hurry, then better to be enjoying Moules Marinière in a French restaurant than tossing about in the tide-troubled Dover Strait as tankers and ferries shave past.

Dover harbour is reasonably safe to enter in most weathers, with one or two provisos. Westerly or south-westerly gales will cause a nasty race off the S breakwater, especially for the 4 hours after HW; in strong southerlies or south-easterlies you get a very confused sea off the W entrance, particularly near LW; and bear in mind that you might be forced to heave-to off the entrance to wait for traffic entering or leaving—it is important, in this case, to keep up-tide as much as possible while you are waiting.

It is not prudent to approach Calais in any onshore winds above Force 6-7. Boulogne has a safer entrance, just over 7 miles S of Cap Gris-Nez, although the tide will be foul for Boulogne if you have set off from Dover to make the best of the NE-going stream for Calais. In heavy weather from between N and NE, a nasty quarter for Calais, you will get some protection from the French coast once you draw S of Gris-Nez.

Because of its new outer breakwaters, Ramsgate is much safer to approach in heavy weather than it used to be. Getting to the entrance can be the tricky part, with the Goodwins forming a grim and notorious cordon to the SE. If, however, you are coming back from Calais in a strong south-westerly, the Goodwins and the coast will give you some lee on the last part of the passage. In a strong north-easterly, you have the option of crossing from Calais to the South Goodwin light-float and passing inside the Goodwins via Gull Stream. You will then get some shelter from the banks up as far as the Brake bell-buoy, but the final approach to the harbour entrance would be rough-going. By taking this route back to Ramsgate, you have the option of turning downwind for Dover as you get near the South Goodwin.

Poor Visibility

Mist or fog is arguably more dangerous than heavy weather in the Dover Strait, given the sheer volume of traffic plying in all directions. Because it is such a congested area though, officers of the watch tend to be glued to their radar screens and there is a good chance of even a small yacht being spotted. Nevertheless, it is sheer lunacy to set off across the Dover Strait traffic separation scheme if you know that poor visibility is likely. If you are caught short by sudden fog banks, your first objective should be to get out of the lanes as soon as possible, whether this means turning back or going on.

As far as navigation goes, Calais is not too difficult to enter in quite murky weather, especially when conditions are calm and you can give full attention to position-fixing. If you are carrying a NE-going tide, try to approach the French coast a couple of miles WSW of CA6 red buoy, in order to avoid the worst of the traffic coming in and out of Calais and so that you can work inshore on the echo-sounder to the S edge of the shipping channel. You can then feel your way E along the 5m line towards the pierheads. Calais main lighthouse has a useful RDF beacon (*305.7kHz, 'CS', 20M, No. 5*), which can be crossed reasonably well with Dunkerque LANBY (*294.2, 'DK', 10M, cont.*). If you are approaching the entrance very close inshore in fog, beware of being carried onto the Jetée Ouest.

If you are wary about the final approach to Calais in poor visibility, you can anchor close inshore in quiet weather, within a couple of miles W of the entrance, so long as you are definitely in shallow water and well to the S of the channel. Not too shallow though—the soundings shoal fairly quickly along this stretch, so make sure that you will stay afloat near LW.

If, on the return passage to Dover, you have set off from Calais and haven't got very far before fog closes in, there is something to be said for returning to the French coast. The tide will probably be carrying you down-Channel and, if the sea is calm, you can aim to make a landfall in the shallow bight to the NE of Cap Gris-Nez. If you are creeping inshore near LW springs though, you need to avoid the shallowest part of Banc à la Ligne, which extends up to 1 mile NE of Gris-Nez. The worst sounding in this vicinity is 0.1 m at LAT and an ordinary spring will give you about 1 m of rise at dead LW.

Approaching Dover in poor visibility is a dangerous business on account of the traffic, and there are no particularly useful anchorages either to the W or the E of the harbour. Provided that the sea is calm, you can home close inshore in very poor visibility towards the South Foreland RDF beacon (*305.7kHz, 'SD', 30M, No. 6*) and anchor right on the 10 m line (don't venture any farther in than this because the depths fall off quickly).

Trying to reach Ramsgate in fog is generally nerve-racking because of the proximity of the Goodwin Sands. If conditions are calm, a useful strategy is to home close inshore on the North Foreland RDF beacon from the ESE (*301.1kHz, 'NF', 50M, cont.*) and then to work S in the shallows between Broadstairs and Ramsgate. A bearing of the Falls light-vessel beacon (*305.7kHz, 'FS', 50M, No. 1*) can give some idea of your progress along this stretch of coast.

High-speed Factors

The 24-mile passage from Dover to Calais makes it perfectly feasible for locally based high-speed motor boats to consider slipping across to France for a leisurely lunch! Most aspects of this crossing covered in the main part of the chapter apply to some extent to motor boats as well as to yachts, although planing craft tend to be more vulnerable to changes in sea conditions which may be brought about by the juxtaposition of wind and tide.

Because the streams are strong in the Dover Strait, it can be preferable to make the crossing during a period of lee-going tide if the wind is at all fresh. However, you may be constrained by having to lock out of Wellington Dock and you would probably also like to catch the opening time for the Bassin de l'Ouest, two factors which are sometimes rather difficult to reconcile. Even if you leave Wellington Dock as soon as possible, say 1½ hours before HW, you can't delay if you want to reach the Calais lock on the same tide. The latest you ought to be passing Calais pierheads is at local HW, which is ½ hour or so after Dover. This gives you a bare two hours for the passage, which has to include some time allowance for ship-dodging.

Both the English and the French coasts show up well on radar. There are Racon beacons on the Varne and Dunkerque LANBYS. Hovercraft make fairly alarming targets on a radar screen, as they whip across the Strait at motorway speeds.

Pilot Books, etc.

Admiralty NP28, *The Dover Strait Pilot*.

North Sea Passage Pilot, B. Navin, 1st edn 1987, published by Imray Laurie Norie and Wilson.

The Shell Pilot to the English Channel, J. Coote, vols 1 and 2, 1987 edns, published by Faber and Faber.

North Sea Harbours: Calais to Den Helder, J. Coote, 6th edn 1988, published by Barnacle Marine.

Adlard Coles Pilot Pack, Vol. 1, B. Goulder, 1st edn 1989, published by Adlard Coles.

The Cruising Association Handbook, 7th edn 1990, published by the Cruising Association.

Admiralty Charts

No. 1892—Dover Strait, western part

No. 323—Dover Strait, eastern part

No. 1828—South Foreland to South Falls Head, including Ramsgate

No. 1352—Approaches to Calais

Tidal Atlases

Admiralty NP233, *Dover Strait*.

Important Lights

English coast:
South Foreland (*Fl3, 20s, 25M*); Dover harbour S breakwater—E Knuckle (*OcWR, 10s, 15M, 13M*), W Head (*OcR, 30s, 18M*); Admiralty pierhead (*Fl, 7½s, 20M; Dia 10s*); Varne LANBY (*FlR, 20s, 22M*); South Goodwin light-float (*Fl2, 30s, 21M*); East Goodwin light-float (*Fl, 15s, 21M*); Ramsgate leading lights in line 270°T—front (*DirOcWRG, 10s, 5M*), rear (*Oc, 5s, 5M*); Ramsgate N breakwater head (*QG, 5M*); Ramsgate S breakwater head (*VQR, 5M*); North Foreland (*Fl5, WR, 20s, 21M, 18M; R vis 150°–200°, W elsewhere*); Falls light-vessel (*Fl2, 10s, 24M*).

French coast:
Sandettié light-vessel (*Fl, 5s, 25M*); Calais main lighthouse (*Fl4, 15s, 23M*); Calais Jetée Est head (*Fl2R, 6s, 17M*); Calais Jetée Ouest head (*IsoG, 3s, 9M*); Cap Gris-Nez (*Fl, 5s, 29M*); Boulogne Digue Nord Head (*FlR, 1½s, 7M*); Boulogne Digue Sud Head (*Fl2+1, 15s, 19M*); Cap d'Alprech (*Fl3, 15s, 23M*).

RDF Beacons

English coast:
Dungeness (*310.3, 'DU', 30M, No. 6*); South Foreland (*305.7, 'SD', 30M, No. 6*); North Foreland (*301.1, 'NF', 50M, cont.*); Falls light-vessel (*305.7, 'FS', 50M, No. 1*).

French coast:
Dunkerque LANBY (*294.2, 'DK', 10M, cont.*); Calais main lighthouse (*305.7, 'CS', 20M, No. 5*); Calais main lighthouse VHF beacon (*Ch. 88, 'CL', 20M, alt with North Foreland*); Cap Gris-Nez (*310.3, 'GN', 30M, Nos. 1, 4*); Cap d'Alprech (*310.3, 'PH', 20M, No. 5*).

Weather Forecasts (all times GMT except where otherwise stated)

BBC shipping forecast area:
　Dover

VHF coast radio stations:
　North Foreland—0803, 2003, on Ch. 26
　Calais—0633, 1133, on Ch. 87

Marinecall:
　Tel. 0898 500 456

Local radio coastal forecasts:
　BBC Radio Kent—Mon–Fri at local times 0645, 0745, 0845, 1231, 1707, 1806; Sat at local times 0815, 0915, 1305; Sun at 0745, 0845, 0945, 1305. Frequencies: *774 and 1035 kHz, 290 and 388 m, 96.7 and 104.2 MHz FM*

Met Office forecasts:
　London Weather Centre, Tel. 01 430 5627

Tidal Streams (times based on HW Dover)

Position	SW-going stream starts	NE-going stream starts
Off Dover W entrance	+0430	−0140
Off Ramsgate harbour entrance	+0415	−0140
Near the Goodwin Knoll buoy	+0545	−0115
1 mile W of Sandettié SW buoy	+0600	−0100
W end of Calais entrance channel	+0440	−0130

Tidal Differences and Heights

Place	Time of HW on Dover	Heights above chart datum in metres			
		MHWS	MLWS	MHWN	MLWN
Dover	–	6.7	0.8	5.3	2.0
Ramsgate	+0020	4.9	0.4	3.8	1.2
Calais	+0035	7.2	1.0	6.0	2.2
Boulogne	+0005	8.9	1.1	7.2	2.8

3 NEWHAVEN TO DIEPPE

The passage from Newhaven or Brighton to Dieppe is probably one of the most straightforward of the English Channel crossings, to the extent that any open-sea passage in a yacht ever seems to be straightforward. It is approximately 63 miles from Newhaven breakwater to Dieppe pierheads, the direct track being 142°T. From Brighton the distance is about 70 miles and the track a few degrees farther E. You reach the W-going shipping lanes only 8 miles S of Beachy Head, and then have about 18 miles to sail before clearing the E-going lane. You may, of course, meet the Newhaven–Dieppe ferries at any time, and they can provide a useful confirmation of your track. The tides in this part of the Channel are moderate, reaching about 2½ knots at springs. The streams flow broadly W by S and E by N, with a pronounced period of slack between each 5½-hour period.

The approaches to Dieppe are uncomplicated, with no off-lying dangers for yachts. The Petits Ecamias and Grands Ecamias banks, which lie respectively 7 and 5 miles NW of Dieppe, are confused in fresh wind-over-tide conditions but both have plenty of water over them. Dieppe is easy to identify in good visibility, with a signal station and church up on the cliffs behind the entrance and a prominent château not quite a mile to the W. In hazy weather you can get some idea of your easting or westing using Pointe d'Ailly RDF beacon, 5 miles W of Dieppe, although there is no other beacon within accurate range to give a good cross.

Dieppe is one of the most agreeable of the cross-Channel ferry ports. Yachts berth just inside the Bassin Duquesne, reached via a lock at the SW corner of the Avant Port. Once through the lock, the pontoon berths are round to starboard behind a short mole. The closer you can tuck in towards the yacht club the better, to avoid the wash from the numerous fishing boats which also use the basin. The yacht club is a friendly spot and the berths are handy for the town centre.

Some 15 miles W along the coast from Dieppe, the small town of St Valéry-en-Caux has a pleasant locked yacht basin which lies only 60 miles from Newhaven. The entrance and outer harbour dry, however, and you need to approach within 2 hours of local HW. It can be dangerous to enter in strong onshore winds and the streams set strongly across the entrance. These constraints complicate a cross-Channel passage direct to St Valéry-en-Caux, whereas Dieppe harbour is accessible at any time and in practically any weather.

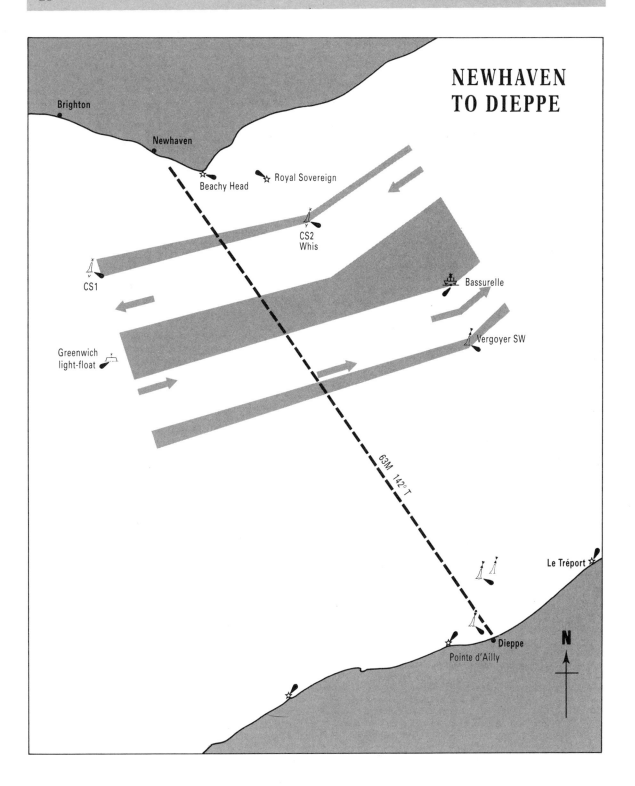

NEWHAVEN TO DIEPPE

Brighton

Newhaven

Beachy Head

Royal Sovereign

CS2
Whis

CS1

Bassurelle

Vergoyer SW

Greenwich
light-float

63M 142° T

Le Tréport

Dieppe

Pointe d'Ailly

N

Le Tréport lies 13 miles E of Dieppe, another harbour which is dangerous to approach in strong onshore winds and where the approaches and Avant Port dry out at LAT. The Bassin à Flot makes rather a dour berth, surrounded as it is by factories and commercial wharves. The lock into this basin is open for about 1½ hours before HW. Watch out for a nasty mudbank just outside the lock on the S side, marked by two unlit buoys.

Heavy Weather

There are worse stretches of water in which to be caught out in heavy weather than this section of the Channel between Newhaven and Dieppe. The coasts are comparatively clear of dangers, the tides are not too strong, shipping is reasonably spaced out although there is rather a shortage of alternative ports of refuge. It is safe to make for Dieppe itself in most conditions, except perhaps in a hard north-westerly if you are not certain of your position along the coast. When approaching in strong onshore winds, try to come in from the NW with the outer pierheads open and the church on the cliffs behind the entrance bearing between 135° and 140°T. Once through the pierheads, come to starboard to hug the line of the W pier, following the harbour S past the ferry terminal (to port) until you reach the Avant Port (to starboard).

In heavy weather from the SW, Newhaven to Dieppe is a rather close reach, allowing for drift, but you should get some lee as you draw towards the French shore. If you can't lay a course for Dieppe, it is an easier slant back to Newhaven. In extreme westerlies or south-westerlies, you have the option of running up-Channel, preferably just S of the E-going lanes. Boulogne is worth keeping in mind, 2½ miles N of Cap d'Alprech and about 8 miles S of Cap Gris-Nez. Boulogne is a feasible refuge in most conditions, but you need to keep 3 miles offshore until the entrance bears E. This line then leads between the offshore shoals, over which the sea breaks dangerously in heavy weather.

Dieppe will be difficult to reach in strong easterlies, although north-easterlies give you a close if unpleasant reach. In any heavy weather from between N and E, there is always the option of freeing off for Cap d'Antifer and making for Le Havre. The coast either side of Cap d'Antifer is straightforward to approach, the light is powerful, and the RDF beacon is useful if the visibility is murky (*291.9kHz, 'TI', 50M, No. 3*). The final approaches to Le Havre are sheltered from the E and NE.

The English coast can be trickier than the French in heavy weather, since it has few alternative destinations. There is no safe harbour E of Newhaven until you reach Dover, nearly 60 miles further up-Channel. To the W you have Brighton Marina, safe to enter under most conditions, but then there is no reliable refuge in onshore winds until you get to the eastern approaches to the Solent, more than 30 miles down-Channel from Brighton.

If, therefore, you are coming back from Dieppe towards Newhaven in strong south-westerlies, it is important to allow generously for drift and keep well up to windward, because you have nowhere to fall back to if Newhaven starts slipping across to the weather bow. In fact, there is much to be said for making for Brighton if the wind allows, because there is then some room in hand if you make more leeway than expected or if the wind should start to veer.

In strong easterlies or north-easterlies, you have the option of freeing off for the Solent, although it is important to make an accurate landfall close E of the Nab Tower in heavy weather, being sure to stay outside the Owers light-float.

Poor Visibility

Shipping is the major headache on this crossing if there is mist or fog about. As long as the sea is calm, it is fairly safe to creep in towards the French coast to the E of Dieppe or within 2 or 3 miles W of it. The 5m line takes you within 4 cables of the coast, but you must definitely anchor or turn left or right if you haven't seen anything by then! Pointe d'Ailly has a useful RDF beacon (*310.3kHz, 'AL', 50M, No. 3*), but it lies nearly 5 miles W of Dieppe and is not safe to home on to because of the various drying rocks which extend for nearly ½-mile seaward of Pointe d'Ailly.

If you don't have Decca, a useful strategy is to make for the E-cardinal bell-buoy which lies 2¾ miles WNW of Dieppe pierheads. As you come within 5 miles of the coast, check the RDF bearing of Pointe d'Ailly to make sure that it is well on your starboard bow. If you hear the bell-buoy and can find it, all well and good; you can then plot the last leg accurately to the harbour entrance. If you miss the buoy, there is no danger in closing the coast so long as Pointe d'Ailly is clearly to the W.

You can carry on creeping shorewards until you are just outside the 5m line; you are then practically on the beach and must either anchor until visibility improves, or turn to port and edge along the coast following the 5m contour. Dieppe west jetty head has a reed fog signal which might help you on the last bit, but you must be continually watching and listening for ships.

Having negotiated the shipping lanes, it is not too difficult to approach the English coast in fog. Royal Sovereign RDF beacon (*310.3kHz, 'RY', 50M, No. 2*) should give some idea of your distance offshore, and you can home towards the low-range RDF beacon on Newhaven W pierhead (*303.4kHz, 'NH', 10M, Nos. 3, 6*). There is also a beacon at Brighton Marina (*303.4kHz, 'BM', 10M, Nos. 2, 5*).

High-speed Factors

This is usually a straightforward passage for power boats, given quiet weather and enough visibility to negotiate the shipping lanes safely. From Newhaven to Dieppe will take just over 4 hours at 15 knots and just over 3 hours at 20 knots, so you could have an early breakfast in Sussex and look forward to lunch in a Normandy restaurant if all goes well.

Streams in this section of the Channel are moderate, so it won't much matter which part of the tidal cycle you choose for the crossing. The main consideration will be the lock times for Dieppe's Bassin Duquesne, because it is not convenient to wait for long in the Avant Port. The Bassin Duquesne is accessible from 2 hours before to 1 hour after local HW (which is almost the same as HW Dover). A good time to arrive off Dieppe is just before HW, when the stream across the harbour entrance will be fairly slack and you should be well placed for the lock. This means clearing Newhaven 3½–4½ hours before HW, which in turn means allowing for an E-going stream throughout the passage.

Skippers of fast motor boats should be wary of north-westerly winds on this passage. It is possible to leave Newhaven in a fresh north-westerly and apparently calm conditions, yet an hour or two later be out in mid-Channel with a hostile sea rearing astern. You may well be reluctant to turn back in this case, but the entrance to Dieppe can be nasty in heavy onshore weather.

The coast near Dieppe shows up well on radar and the cliffs near Beachy Head make a good target for the return trip. The Racon beacon on the Greenwich LANBY will be right at the limit of its nominal range on this passage ('T', 15M).

Pilot Books, etc.

Admiralty NP28, *The Dover Strait Pilot.*

Adlard Coles Pilot pack, Vol. 1, B. Goulder, 1st edn 1989, published by Adlard Coles.

The Shell Pilot to the English Channel, J. Coote, vols 1 and 2, 1987 edns, published by Faber and Faber.

Normandy and Channel Island Pilot, M. Brackenbury, 7th edn 1988, published by Adlard Coles.

North France Pilot, T. and D. Thompson, 1st edn 1989, published by Imray Laurie Norie and Wilson.

Admiralty Charts

No. 2675—English Channel

No. 1652—Selsey Bill to Beachy Head

No. 2612—Cap d'Antifer to Pointe du Haut Banc

No. 2147—Approaches to Dieppe

Tidal Atlases

Admiralty NP250, *English and Bristol Channels.*

Stanford's Tidal Atlas, English Channel East (recommended).

Important Lights

English coast:

Newhaven breakwater (*Oc2, 10s, 12M*); Newhaven East Pier (*IsoG, 5s, 6M*); Beachy Head (*Fl2, 20s, 24M*); Royal Sovereign light-float (*Fl, 20s, 15M*); Greenwich 44 LANBY (*Fl, 5s, 21M*).

French coast:

Pointe d'Ailly (*Fl3, 20s, 30M*); Dieppe—Jetée Est head (*Oc4R, 12s, 8M*), Jetée Ouest head (*IsoWG, 4s, 12M, 8M; W 095°-164°T, G 164°-095°T but obscured by Pointe d'Ailly when bearing less than 080°T*); St Valéry-en-Caux—Jetée Est head (*Fl2R, 6s*), Jetée Ouest head (*Oc1+2G, 12s, 14M*); Le Tréport—Jetée Est head (*OcR, 4s, 7M*), Jetée Ouest head (*Fl2G, 10s, 24M*); Ault lighthouse (*Oc3WR, 12s, 18M, 14M; W 040°-175°T, R 175°-220°T*); Cayeux (*FlR, 5s, 22M*); Pointe du Hourdel (*Oc3WG, 12s, 11M, 9M; W 053°-248°T, G 248°-323° T*); St Valéry-sur-Somme—embankment head (*Fl3G, 6s, 3M*), mole head (*FlR, 4s, 8M*).

RDF Beacons

English coast:

Newhaven west pier (*303.4, 'NH', 10M, Nos. 3, 6*);

Brighton Marina (*303.4, 'BM', 10M, Nos. 2, 5*); Royal Sovereign (*310.3, 'RY', 50M, No. 2*); Dungeness (*310.3, 'DU', 30M, No. 6*).

French coast:

Pointe d'Ailly (*310.3, 'AL', 50M, No. 3*); Cap d'Antifer (*291.9, 'TI', 50M, No. 3*).

Weather Forecasts (all times GMT except where otherwise stated)

BBC shipping forecast area:

Wight

VHF coast radio stations:

Hastings—0803, 2003, on Ch. 7

Dieppe—0633, 1133, on Ch. 2

Marinecall:

Tel. 0898 500 456

Local radio coastal forecasts:

None specially for mariners

Met Office forecasts:

Southampton Weather Centre, Tel. 0703 228844

Tidal Streams (times based on HW Dover)

Position	W-going stream starts	E-going stream starts
Off Newhaven entrance	+0030	−0615
2 miles S of Beachy Head	+0100	−0515
Mid-Channel between Newhaven and Dieppe	+0100	−0440
3 miles NW of Dieppe entrance	+0120	−0440

Tidal Differences and Heights

Place	Time of HW on Dover	Heights above chart datum in metres			
		MHWS	MLWS	MHWN	MLWN
Newhaven	HW	6.6	0.5	5.2	1.9
Brighton	+0005	6.5	0.6	5.1	1.9
Dieppe	−0010	9.1	0.6	7.1	2.4
St Valéry-en-Caux	−0025	8.7	0.8	7.0	2.3
Le Tréport	−0005	9.2	0.6	7.3	2.3
St Valéry-sur-Somme	+0025	9.8	–	7.9	–

4 SOLENT TO
THE SEINE

The broad estuary of the Seine can seem rather forbidding 'on paper' to anyone planning a passage and landfall from the S coast of England. This impression is only partly justified, and yet the general picture has something in common with the approaches to several other of the great European rivers—shoal water prone to a short steep chop on a weather-going tide, many sandbanks, strongish local streams, and a tendency towards poor visibility to confound an already limited selection of landmarks. The atmosphere is not improved, as you study the chart, by the alarming number of wrecks scattered about.

Take heart, though. *The Channel Pilot*, not normally inclined to make light of navigational difficulties, is comparatively optimistic and matter-of-fact about this corner of Normandy: 'Estuaire de la Seine is entered between Pointe de Beuzeval, 6½ cables north-eastward of Dives light-structure, and Cap de la Hève, 13½ miles north-north-eastward. It is encumbered by shifting banks, which are prolonged seaward by Banc de Seine. Access to the estuary is easy and it is well marked . . .' It continues: 'The white limestone cliffs in the vicinity of Cap de la Hève are visible from a great distance when the sun shines on them; thence the cliffs on the northern side of the estuary as far as Cap d'Antifer, 11 miles north-eastward, are reddish in colour.'

The mouth of the Seine faces W, with the port of Le Havre dominating its N shore. The small fishing harbour of Honfleur lies 7 miles above Le Havre on the S side of the estuary. Le Havre is accessible at all states of tide and the large Port du Plaisance offers a comfortable enough berth for visitors. Honfleur is much more picturesque and restful than Le Havre, but may only be entered with sufficient rise of tide; the lock into the Vieux Bassin operates for about an hour either side of HW.

Many yachts calling at either Le Havre or Honfleur are bound up the Seine, either for a short exploratory visit or on their way well inland to join the canal system and pick up one of the routes to the Mediterranean. Those planning a brief foray will find the lower reaches of the river most attractive, although the current is powerful and you are likely to come across a significant amount of substantial commercial traffic. You can get all the way to Rouen with your mast stepped, but Paris may only be reached by transforming your proud craft into a low-profile motor boat.

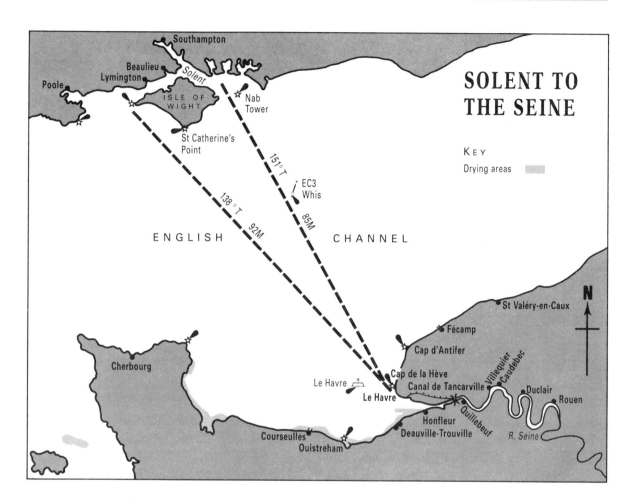

Passage Planning

It is 85 miles at 151°T from the Spithead forts to Le Havre channel entrance. Yachts from most of the Solent harbours or from Portsmouth will use this track, which leads ¾ mile E of Bembridge Ledge buoy, not quite 2½ miles W of the Nab Tower, out towards the main shipping lanes and 3½ miles W of separation buoy EC3.

Yachts coming from Langstone or Chichester harbours will probably take their departure further E, somewhere between the Nab and the Bullock Patch buoy. In this case, depending on the tide, you

will pass closer to EC3, perhaps within 1 mile or so. Over on the French side of the Channel, the direct track leads 12 or 13 miles W of Cap d'Antifer before you begin to close the land off Cap de la Hève. A deep-water lane extends 35 miles WNW from Port d'Antifer oil terminal and so, while you are still some way offshore, you can expect to meet large tankers using this route, or other shipping heading to or from Le Havre or the Seine.

In clear visibility, the coast between Cap d'Antifer and Cap de la Hève is easy to identify, with the two headlands and lighthouses being well placed for bearings as you approach Le Havre. Other useful landmarks are a conspicuous water-tower 5 miles NNE of Cap de la Hève and a radio mast a couple of miles S of Cap d'Antifer. As you come down towards La Hève, you will see two tall chimneys among Le Havre's dockland, which should be directly ahead when you turn into the buoyed entrance channel on about 107°T.

This 6-mile corridor is dredged for shipping and leads towards Le Havre from the direction of the Le Havre LANBY. Yachts need not pick up the buoys at the seaward end and I would aim to join near LH5 and 6, about 3 miles W by S from Cap de la Hève. Keep well to the S side and clear of all commercial traffic.

By making for this particular pair of buoys, roughly half-way along the outer part of the channel, you maximize the chance of spotting something if the visibility were to deteriorate as you approach the estuary. This strategy should keep you in safe water, even if your navigation is a couple of miles in error E or W and provided that you can see at least ½ mile. In any case, strangers ought to join the channel seaward of buoys LH9 and LH10, especially near low tide, since the shoals on either side of the entrance channel lie to the E of this gateway.

Setting the Course

Because the longitude of Le Havre is well E of the Nab Tower, it is preferable to carry more E-going Channel tide than W-going. If you average 5 knots, the passage from Spithead to Le Havre entrance should take approximately 17 hours. Other things being equal, it might therefore be best to be passing No Man's Land Fort just as the up-Channel tide is starting, about 6 hours before HW Dover.

However, you also have the tides in the Solent itself to consider. At 6 hours before HW Dover,

the stream will have been trickling SE from the Bramble for nearly 2 hours and ebbing down Southampton Water for about 5 hours. Anyone coming from, say, Cowes, the Hamble, Hythe, Ocean Village, or farther up the Test or Itchen, will thus be able to take advantage of both the local and the Channel tides.

Yachts based in Langstone or Chichester harbours have their own tidal constraints to contend with, but can make considerable use of the main Channel stream by crossing their respective bars a little before half-tide down—sea conditions permitting. Those coming from the far W of the Solent may well decide to slip out through the Needles Channel on the last of the ebb, turning to the SE just as the Channel flood is starting and setting a course to make good 138°T for the 92 miles to Le Havre entrance.

Entering the Seine Directly

By leaving the Solent on the first of the main E-going stream and averaging 5 knots over the passage, you would be arriving off the Seine estuary on the last of the *next* E-going cycle, that is, close to HW at Le Havre. This is fine for entering Le Havre itself, but rather too late if you plan to go straight into the river via the Chenal de Rouen and make for Honfleur. It is exactly the *wrong* timing if your intention is to continue directly upstream.

The most convenient time to arrive at Honfleur is about 1 hour before local HW, in order to catch the lock into the Vieux Bassin. This means reaching the NW Ratier green buoy 2½ hours before local HW. This buoy and its red twin form the outer gate to the well-marked Chenal de Rouen, which leads E into the river towards Honfleur, leaving the Digue du Ratier and its various beacons to starboard.

The tide in the estuary will be fair at this time, with

plenty of water in the Honfleur approach channel. Working back from this schedule, you would need to be in the vicinity of the LH5 and 6 buoys about 3½ hours before local HW, which would put your required departure from Spithead Forts at something like 3 hours after HW Dover, or just before half-ebb at Portsmouth.

The Passage to Rouen

Given a 5-knot cruising speed, it is quite feasible to enter the Seine and make good the 70 miles to Rouen on one tide. Because the time of HW gets progressively later farther upriver, you can carry a fair stream for most of the 10 hours that the passage will take. You need to arrive off the NW Ratier buoy just before LW Le Havre; the ebb is still running out of the river then, but the new flood will be starting in an hour or so.

The 'Seine Maritime' is fairly straightforward, as long as you press on, keep clear of ships, and don't attempt to navigate at night. It can be dangerous to moor anywhere near the bank, even alongside seemingly secure quays. Not only is there often less water than you would think, but the strong current and the wash from passing ships will make life extremely difficult. If you cannot reach Rouen in one hop, either because you started late on the tide or daylight is running short, there are safe waiting moorings at Quillebeuf, Villequier, Caudebec and Duclair.

Heavy Weather on Passage

The crossing from the Solent to the Seine is distinctly lacking in bad-weather options. The only consolation is that, should the wind freshen from the SW while you are on passage, it gives you a close reach rather than a dead noser; you will also obtain increasing shelter as you close the French coast. Arriving off the Seine in heavy weather, it is almost always safer to make for Le Havre than to try and negotiate the river entrance.

If heavy westerly weather sets you E of Le Havre, the choice of bolt-holes is not encouraging. Fécamp lies 9 miles ENE along the coast from Cap d'Antifer, but its narrow entrance is only dredged to 1–1½ m. The approaches shelve steeply and can be nasty in strong W or NW winds. Once inside the harbour, the pontoon berths provide good shelter, although deepish draught boats may touch bottom near LW. St Valéry-en-Caux lies 15 miles ENE of Fécamp, its narrow drying entrance accessible for about 2½ hours either side of HW but dangerous in strong onshore winds. The inner part of the harbour has been converted into a pleasant locked marina.

The situation is no better to the W of Le Havre. The only harbours of note along the S shore of the Baie de Seine are Courseulles, Ouistreham, and Deauville-Trouville (which is close to Le Havre in any case). None of these is suitable as a port of refuge, although Ouistreham can be entered at any state of tide.

Keep Cherbourg in mind if you are unlucky enough to encounter heavy weather from between E and SE. It will lie at least 50 miles off your direct track though, and is therefore something of a last resort if you need to come off the wind but prefer to make for France rather than stay at sea or return to the Solent.

Poor Visibility

In poor visibility, it is usually safer to make for Le Havre than to try and enter the Seine. The coast between Cap d'Antifer and Cap de la Hève presents no great danger in quiet weather, the depths shelving steadily as you close the land. My tactic in fog is to make for channel buoys LH5 and 6 as planned, and then to use the changing bearing of Le Havre LANBY RDF beacon to indicate southward progress. If you are really groping in murk, the back-bearing of this beacon will help you towards the harbour entrance while you hope to pick up one of the buoys. Shipping will represent the greatest hazard as you make this approach.

The Return Passage

One feature of this Channel crossing is that a nice settled north-westerly, which is ideal for the outward trip, is almost a headwind for the return passage. The East Solent landfall is pretty straightforward and most yachts make for a position near the Nab Tower. In poor visibility, you can home right up to the Nab by RDF and then use its back-bearing as you enter the Solent.

High-speed Factors

This is a longish passage—85 miles from the Spithead forts to Le Havre entrance channel, so at least 100 miles from most of the Solent harbours 'door-to-door'. It can be useful for fast power boats to use the English Channel buoy EC3 as an intermediate waypoint, especially since it has a Racon beacon ('T', 10M).

Your arrival at Le Havre is not critical as far as tides are concerned, because the Port de Plaisance du Havre is accessible at any time, by day or night. Most skippers will prefer to make the whole passage in daylight, so the main factor to bear in mind is the direction of the Channel stream in relation to the wind. You will have a quieter trip if the tide is E-going in westerly winds or W-going in easterlies.

A convenient landfall waypoint is a position near LH6 or LH8 Le Havre approach buoys, and then you can cross the fairway and follow the S line of buoys to the harbour entrance. About 25 miles from Le Havre you cross the deep-water channel which leads to Port d'Antifer oil terminal, so you need to watch out for large ships in this area and, indeed, in the approaches to Le Havre itself. You can, if you like, use one of the Port d'Antifer channel buoys as another intermediate waypoint, probably the A5 W-cardinal buoy about 18 miles WNW of Cap d'Antifer. The high coast between Cap d'Antifer and Cap de la Hève shows up well on radar and Le Havre LANBY has a Racon beacon of 8–10 miles range.

Pilot Books, etc.

Admiralty NP27, *The Channel Pilot.*

Admiralty NP74, *List of Lights, Vol. A.*

The Shell Pilot to the English Channel, J. Coote, vols 1 and 2, 1987 edns, published by Faber and Faber.

Normandy and Channel Island Pilot, M. Brackenbury, 7th edn 1988, published by Adlard Coles.

The Cruising Association Handbook, 7th edn 1990, published by the Cruising Association.

A Cruising Guide to the Lower Seine, E. L. Howells, published by Imray Laurie Norie and Wilson.

Charts

Admiralty:

No. 2675—English Channel

No. 2045—Outer Approaches to the Solent

No. 2050—Eastern Approaches to the Solent

No. 394—The Solent, Eastern Part

No. 2613—Cherbourg to Cap d'Antifer

No. 2146—Approaches to Le Havre

No. 2990—Le Havre and Approaches to La Seine

No. 2994—La Seine; Honfleur to Rouen

Imray:

C3—Isle of Wight

C12—Eastern English Channel Passage Chart

C32—Baie de la Seine

Stanford:

No. 1—English Channel, Eastern Section (rather a small scale, so better to use Admiralty No. 2675 or Imray C12)

Tidal Atlases

Stanford's Tidal Atlas, *English Channel East* (recommended).

Admiralty NP250, *English and Bristol Channels.*

Note: A useful set of tidal charts for the Seine estuary is given in the Le Havre section of the Admiralty *Channel Pilot.*

Tidal Streams (times based on HW Dover)

Position	E-going stream starts	W-going stream starts
Spithead forts	+0345	−0125
Close off the Nab Tower	+0550	−0015
Close W of EC3 buoy	−0545	+0015
12 miles due W of Cap d'Antifer	−0500	+0050
Entrance to Chenal de Rouen	−0605	−0005

Tidal Differences and Heights

Place	Time of HW on Dover	Heights above chart datum in metres			
		MHWS	MLWS	MHWN	MLWN
Cowes, Isle of Wight	+0030	4.2	0.6	3.5	1.7
Portsmouth	+0030	4.7	0.6	3.8	1.8
Bembridge	+0030	3.1	–	2.3	–
Le Havre	−0105	7.8	1.0	6.4	2.7
Honfleur	−0130	7.8	–	6.4	–

Important Lights

English coast:

No Man's Land Fort (*Fl, 5s, 15M*); Horse Sand Fort (*Fl, 10s, 15M*); St Helen's Fort (*Fl3, 10s, 8M*); Nab Tower (*Fl2, 10s, 19M*); Owers lighthouse buoy (*Fl3, 20s, 22M*); St Catherine's Point (*Fl, 5s, 20M*); Separation buoy EC3 (*FlY, 5s, whis*).

French coast:

Cap d'Antifer (*Fl, 20s, 26M*); Cap de la Hève (*Fl, 5s, 26M*); Le Havre LANBY (*Fl2R, 10s, 20M*); Banc de Seine platform (*2Mo'U', 15s, 13M*); Pointe de Ver (*Fl3, 15s, 26M*); Le Havre 'Digue Nord' (*FlR, 5s, 21M*); Le Havre 'Digue Sud' (*VQ3G, 2s, 13M*); Entrance to Chenal de Rouen, Digue du Ratier Head, Platform 'A' (*VQ, 8M*); Falaise des Fonds (*Fl3, WRG, 12s, 14M, 11M, 11M; W vis 100°-109°T; R vis 080°-084°T, 109°-162°T; G vis 040°-080°T, 084°-100°T, 162°-260°T*); Honfleur 'Digue Ouest' Head (*QG, 5M*); Honfleur 'Digue Est' Head (*QFl, 8M*); Honfleur mole head (*Oc2R, 6s*).

RDF Beacons

English coast:

St Catherine's Point (*291.9kHz, 'CP', 50M, No.2*); High Down Scratchells Bay VHF beacon (*VHF Ch. 88, 'HD', 30M, alt with 'AL'*); Nab Tower (*312.6kHz, 'NB', 10M, Nos. 1, 3, 5*); Chichester Bar beacon (*303.4kHz, 'CH', 10M, Nos. 1, 4*).

French coast:

Cap d'Antifer (*291.9kHz, 'TI', 50M, No. 3*); Pointe de Barfleur (*291.9kHz, 'FG', 70M, No. 6*); Pointe de Ver (*291.9kHz, 'éR', 20M, No. 5*); Le Havre LANBY (*291.9kHz, 'LH', 30M, No. 4*).

Weather Forecasts (all times GMT except where otherwise stated)

BBC shipping forecast area:

Wight

VHF coast radio stations:

Niton—0833, 2003, on Ch. 28

Le Havre—0633, 1133, on Ch. 82

Marinecall:

Tel. 0898 500 456/457

Local radio coastal forecasts:

BBC Radio Solent—Mon–Fri at local time 0745; Sat at 0730, 0835,1259, 1402, 1533, 1925; Sun at 0835, 0850, 0930, 1030, 1304, 1504. Frequencies: *999 and 1359 kHz, 221 and 300m, 96.1 MHz FM*

Met Office forecasts:

Southampton Weather Centre, Tel. 0703 228844

5 THE NEEDLES TO CHERBOURG

The 60-mile stretch of English Channel that lies between Cherbourg breakwaters and the inimitable chalk stacks of the Needles is probably one of the most well-trodden sailing routes around Britain. It is sometimes regarded as a 'milk-run', just the thing for a long weekend from the Solent harbours, although to contemplate any open-sea passage too lightly is always tempting providence. In fact, this crossing is not without its hazards, despite the frequency with which it is undertaken each season.

The powerful tidal streams provide the main navigational complication, especially towards the French side of the Channel. Peak spring rates can reach 4–5 knots, but even the more modest 2–3 knots between springs and neaps is not exactly negligible. You need to calculate the likely *net set* with some care when planning this passage; it is generally not accurate enough simply to say 'six hours one way, six hours the other, so it will probably cancel out . . .' It often doesn't.

The course from the Bridge W-cardinal buoy to Cherbourg's Fort de l'Ouest is 182°T, but there are some strategic questions to keep in mind when deciding on your ideal track. These revolve around what the tide and weather are likely to be doing as

you approach the French coast. It is a good idea to try and keep some easting or westing in reserve, depending on which of the elements you think will have the upper hand as you make your landfall.

As far as the rise of tide is concerned, it doesn't much matter when you arrive at Cherbourg—the harbour and yacht marina are accessible at any state of tide, by day or night. On the English side, though, you need a fair stream for coming out of Hurst Narrows and the Needles Channel, and this will probably be the main constraint on your departure time. Weekenders will want to try and get away as soon as possible on a Friday evening, but if the crossing to Cherbourg is the first leg of a longer cruise, most yachtsmen will aim to make the whole passage in daylight.

If the wind is at all fresh from the W or SW, it is best to negotiate the 4 miles between Hurst and the Bridge buoy in the hour before HW Dover, just as the weather-going stream is about to start. By thus slipping out on the very first of the ebb, you should avoid the steep wind-over-tide chop that can soon build up in the W entrance of the Solent.

How feasible this is depends on which part of the Solent you are leaving from. Yarmouth is usually the handiest port of departure, although Lyming-

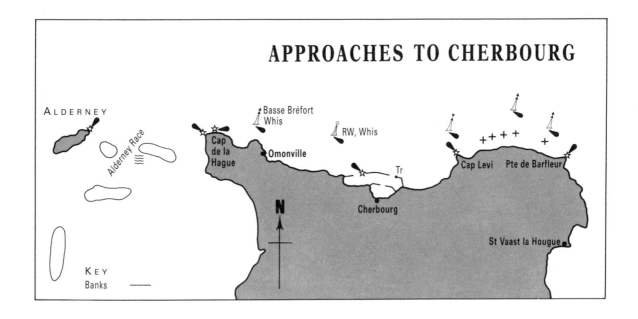

APPROACHES TO CHERBOURG

ALDERNEY

Alderney Race

Basse Bréfort
Whis

RW, Whis

Cap
de la
Hague

Omonville

Tr

Cap Levi

Pte de Barfleur

Cherbourg

N

St Vaast la Hougue

KEY
Banks ———

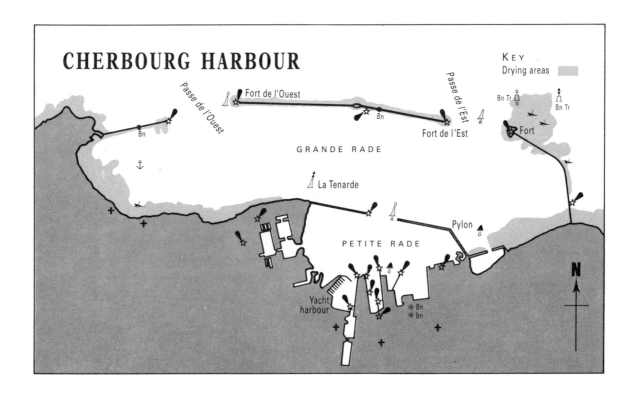

CHERBOURG HARBOUR

KEY
Drying areas

Passe de l'Ouest

Fort de l'Ouest

Passe de l'Est

Bn Tr

Bn Tr

Bn

Bn

Fort de l'Est

Fort

GRANDE RADE

La Tenarde

Pylon

PETITE RADE

Yacht
harbour

Bn

Bn

N

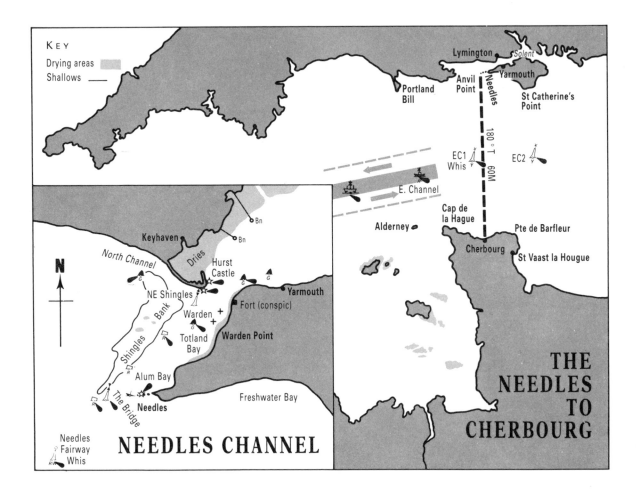

ton is also fairly well placed for Hurst. However, coming from farther E, you'll need to carry part of the W-going stream down the Solent, so the Narrows will be well stirred up by the time you get there. In quiet or easterly weather, of course, there is no problem in taking the Needles Channel at any time during the ebb.

An Ideal Start

Imagine a peaceful summer morning in Yarmouth and you are sitting in the cockpit early, waiting for the 0555 shipping forecast. It looks like the begin-

ning of a perfect day, a slight haze boding well for continuing sunshine. A gentle north-westerly is just stirring the harbour, probably indicating a moderate breeze at sea. You slipped into Yarmouth yesterday evening from the Hamble, having pushed the last of the flood down the Solent.

You are just starting a fortnight's cruise to the Channel Islands area and plan to make for Cherbourg first. You could have carried on to sea last night, since the tide was turning fair and the weather looked satisfactory, but you only drove down from the office that afternoon, having had a hectic couple of days in preparation for going away.

Caution prevailed and you opted for a full night's sleep in Yarmouth and a daylight passage today. The tides will be just as convenient for the Needles Channel this morning, the weather seems set fair and the barometer is rising slowly.

The forecast confirms this decision, giving north-westerlies Force 3–4, with moderate visibility becoming good later. HW Dover is at 0745 BST, so casting off from Yarmouth soon after 0630 should be about right. The first of the W-going stream will be just starting to run in Yarmouth Roads as you clear the harbour entrance, but Hurst Narrows will still be more or less slack.

Setting a Course

It is 5½ miles from Yarmouth to the Bridge buoy which, allowing for some favourable tide, should take about 1 hour at 5 knots; you might therefore plan your departure from the Bridge at 0730. Now the tides are neaps when HW Dover is at this time in the morning, which is really what you want for this passage given the choice. The height of HW Dover might be something like 5.6 m, so if, like me, you use the excellent *Stanford's Tidal Atlas*, this is the figure you would enter in the spring/neap conversion tables. Using this atlas and assuming 5 knots cruising speed, you would predict a westerly set of about 8½ miles for the first 6 hours and an easterly set of 7½ miles for the second 6 hours.

With a net westerly set of 1 mile, your course to steer for Cherbourg W entrance would come out at pretty much due S true. Now having worked through this calculation the night before your passage, and actually arrived at the Bridge on the morning in question, you would have to weigh up various less predictable factors to do with weather and your likely progress, and then make a final judgement about which course you will actually

steer. If you average less than 5 knots, for example, the passage will take more than 12 hours, and you'll be picking up the new W-going stream as you arrive off Cherbourg. If this looks likely, you should set a course a little to the E of S, to allow room to fall back with the tide as you make your landfall.

If you average *more* than 5 knots, the trip will take less than 12 hours and you'll obtain greater influence from westerly set than from easterly. If this looks like being the case, there might again be some advantage in setting a course to the E of S—perhaps a less important precaution than in the previous case because, by making an early landfall W of Cherbourg, you will arrive up-tide of your destination and can easily bear away for the harbour entrance.

Should the wind turn out to be westerly rather than north-westerly, you might decide to hold up 5 degrees or so, to allow for any leeway or surface drift, or simply as a precaution against the wind backing *en route*. However, if all went according to plan, and having kept a course of 180°T, you should pass 1 mile or so to the W of the traffic separation buoy EC1 soon after 1400. This buoy will provide a useful mid-Channel check on your tidal set.

Continuing southward, you ought to arrive off Cherbourg's Fort de l'Ouest at about 1930, just as the E-going stream is falling slack. It would still be daylight for locating and negotiating the main entrance—the Passe de l'Ouest—and then working the last 2½ miles across the Grande Rade to the Petite Rade and into the marina.

Poor Visibility

Cherbourg is relatively straightforward to approach in poor visibility, as long as you have made a reasonably accurate allowance for tidal set. Other things being equal, you should err on the side of a landfall to the W of Cherbourg rather than to the E, because the coast is much cleaner in this direction. The RDF beacon on Fort de l'Ouest has a useful 20-mile range (*312.6kHz, 'RB', 20M, Nos. 2, 4, 6*) and it is quite safe to home right up to it from northward.

Cherbourg CH1 fairway whistle buoy lies not quite 3 miles 350°T from Fort de l'Ouest, so the reciprocal of 170°T makes a good homing track for the Fort in fog, giving you a chance of spotting or hearing the buoy as you close the coast. Probably the most significant danger in closing Cherbourg in poor visibility lies in meeting ships and ferries entering or leaving the harbour.

Bad Weather *en route*?

Cherbourg provides a secure refuge in almost any weather and is accessible whatever the tide, by day or night. Skippers of yachts bound for the Channel Islands from south coast ports are always pleased to have Cherbourg to make for if conditions harden from the SW—the land between Cap de la Hague and Fort de l'Ouest offers increasing shelter as you approach the entrance.

However, if Cherbourg is your intended destination and the weather is likely to deteriorate, you need to plan your track strategically to be sure of being able to reach one of the harbour entrances if the wind should shift and freshen. The classic catch is a passage made in westerlies when a yacht finds herself 15 or 20 miles short of Cherbourg at spring tides, being set more powerfully eastward than anticipated. At the same time, a warm front moves up-Channel, the wind increases and backs SW, and it becomes impossible to lay a course for Cherbourg or to beat up towards it.

If you find yourself in that position, you have the option of bearing away round Pointe de Barfleur

and then heading for the marina at St Vaast le Hougue, 6 miles S of that headland. In poor visibility, make sure that you *are* rounding Barfleur and not closing the bleak and rocky stretch of coast to the E of Cap Levi. The Barfleur RDF beacon is useful here (*291.9kHz, 'FG', 70M, No. 6*).

Give a good berth to Barfleur race which, at springs, extends for 3 or 4 miles NE and E of the headland. At the same time, try not to round Pointe de Barfleur by too great a distance or you will lose the valuable shelter afforded by the weather shore—you'll also have to fight up to windward to reach St Vaast.

The port of Barfleur lies 1½ miles S of Pointe de Barfleur. The harbour dries and is not an ideal port of refuge, especially with St Vaast marina so close. St Vaast is a large yacht haven with pontoon berths for up to 150 visitors. Entry is by way of a lock gate from about 2½ hours before to 3½ hours after local HW.

In different circumstances, remember that the small harbour of Omonville lies 8 miles WNW of Cherbourg W entrance. You can stay afloat here, protected from seaward by a stone pier. Omonville can be handy if you find yourself W of Cherbourg with the tide turning foul, but the harbour is open to the E.

The Return Passage

As with the outward leg, the return trip from Cherbourg to the Needles involves taking careful account of tidal set. When planning the passage, you should aim to be a cautious distance up-tide of the Needles Fairway buoy as you make your landfall. The Needles Channel is an effective tidal gate, so you need to arrive at the Bridge buoy with sufficient E-going stream in hand to carry you at least beyond Hurst Narrows as far as Yarmouth.

The VHF beacons at Anvil Point and Scratchells Bay are a great help when closing the Needles in poor visibility. Their directional transmitters alternate on VHF Ch. 88, with a nominal range of 14 and 30 miles respectively. As you get close in, the Needles lighthouse has a good piercing foghorn (*2 ev 30s*).

High-speed Factors

Cherbourg? Turn left at the Needles and then head due S for 60 miles, you can't miss it. Can't you indeed? Despite the frequency with which this passage is undertaken each season, it is remarkably easy to misjudge the tides and end up being set well to the W or E of your intended landfall. In the old days, you wouldn't have known until you found yourself down off Cap de la Hague or somewhere between Cap Levi and Barfleur, but Decca now helps us to correct any miscalculations in good time.

The streams are strong between the Needles and Cherbourg, so you need to do your homework before setting off. The departure is also likely to depend upon the forecast strength and direction of the wind. In westerlies, you will have a quieter passage by taking the middle hours of the E-going Channel stream, and vice versa. Assuming you can average 15–20 knots, this would mean clearing the Needles fairway buoy 5–6 hours before HW Dover in westerly weather, or soon after HW Dover in easterly weather.

The direct track of 180°T leads 6 miles E of the English Channel buoy EC1, which has a Racon beacon (*'T', 90s, 10M*). This can give you a mid-Channel fix, but it is not really worth using EC1 as an intermediate waypoint, unless you happen to time your passage so that the tide carries you W for the first half of the passage and then back E as you approach Cherbourg.

The coast either side of Cherbourg provides a reasonable radar target, with Cherbourg harbour showing first as a fairly wide gap between Nacqueville hill to the W and the high ground behind Cap Levi to the E.

Most motor-boat skippers will not set off unless they are pretty sure of being able to reach Cherbourg safely. However, in freshening weather from the W or SW, there is always the option of easing off to round Pointe de Barfleur and making for the sheltered marina at St Vaast la Hougue.

Pilot Books, etc.

Admiralty NP27, *The Channel Pilot.*

Admiralty NP74, *List of Lights, Vol. A.*

Channel Harbours and Anchorages, K. Adlard Coles, 6th edn 1985, published by Nautical.

The Shell Pilot to the English Channel, J. Coote, vols 1 and 2, 1987 edns, published by Faber and Faber.

The Cruising Association Handbook, 7th edn 1990, published by the Cruising Association.

Normandy and Channel Island Pilot, M. Brackenbury, 7th edn (revised) 1990, published by Adlard Coles.

Adlard Coles Pilot Pack, Vol. 2, B. Goulder, 1st edn 1989, published by Adlard Coles.

Charts

Admiralty:

No. 2675—The English Channel

No. 2615—Bill of Portland to the Needles

No. 2045—Outer approaches to the Solent

No. 2219—Western approaches to the Solent

No. 2040—The Solent, western part, including Yarmouth harbour

No. 1106—Approaches to Cherbourg

No. 2602—Cherbourg

No. 1349—Barfleur and St Vaast la Hougue

Imray:

C3—Isle of Wight

C10—Western English Channel Passage Chart

C33A—Channel Islands, North

C42—Baie de la Seine

Stanford:

No. 7—English Channel, Central Section

No. 11—The Solent, Needles to Selsey Bill

Tidal Atlases

Stanford's Tidal Atlas, English Channel West (recommended).

Admiralty NP250, *English and Bristol Channels.*

Admiralty NP337, *The Solent and adjacent waters.*

Tidal Streams (times based on HW Dover)

Position	E-going stream starts	W-going stream starts
Hurst Narrows	+0530	−0050
1 mile W of the Needles	+0545	−0015
30 miles S of the Needles	+0615	−0020
5 miles N of Cherbourg	+0545	−0045
Close inshore W of Cherbourg	+0530	−0230

Tidal Differences and Heights

Place	Time of HW on Dover	Heights above chart datum in metres			
		MHWS	MLWS	MHWN	MLWN
Yarmouth, Isle of Wight	−0035 and	3.1	0.6	−	1.4
	+0120 (springs)	2.8	−	−	−
	+0035 (neaps)	−	−	2.5	−
Cherbourg	−0340	6.2	0.8	4.8	2.3
Omonville	−0350	6.1	0.8	4.7	2.4
Barfleur	−0240	6.4	0.9	5.1	2.3
St Vaast la Hougue	−0240	6.0	0.6	5.1	2.1

Important Lights

English coast:

The Needles (*Oc2, 20s, WRG, 17M, 14M, 14M*); Anvil Point (*Fl, 10s, 24M, vis 237°–076°T*); St Catherine's Point (*Fl, 5s, 30M, vis 257°–117°T; FR, 17M, vis 099°–116°T*); Hurst Point, Needles Channel leading lights in line 042°T—Low light (*Iso, 4s, 14M, vis 029°–053°T*), High light (*Iso, 6s, WR, 14M; W vis 080°–104°T, 234°–244°T, 250°–053°T; R vis 244°–250°T*); Needles Fairway buoy (*LFl, 10s*); Yarmouth Harbour leading lights in line 188°T—front (*2FG, 2M*), rear (*FG, 2M*).

French coast:

Cap de la Hague, Rocher Gros du Raz (*Fl, 5s, 24M, vis 354°–274°T*); Cap de la Hague, La Plate (*Fl, 2+1, WR, 12s, 9M, 6M; W vis 115°–272°T, R vis 272°–115°T*); Cherbourg Fort de l'Ouest (*Fl3, WR, 15s, 23M, 19M; W vis 122°–355°T, R vis 355°–122°T*); Cherbourg Fort de l'Est (*IsoWG, 4s, 10M, 6M; W vis 008°–229°T, R vis 229°–008°T*); Cap Levi (*FlR, 5s, 20M*); Pointe de Barfleur (*Fl2, 10s, 27M*); Port de Barfleur leading lights in line 219°T, synchronized (*Oc3, 12s, 10M*).

RDF Beacons

English coast:

Portland Bill (*291.9kHz, 'PB', 50M, No. 1*); St Catherine's Point (*291.9kHz, 'CP', 50M, No. 2*); Hurn aero beacon (*322kHz, 'HRN', 15M, cont.*); Anvil Point VHF beacon (*VHF Ch. 88, 'AL', 14M, alt with 'HD'*); High Down Scratchells Bay VHF beacon (*VHF Ch. 88, 'HD', 30M, alt with 'AL'*).

French coast and N. Channel Islands:

Casquets lighthouse (*298.8kHz, 'QS', 50M, No. 3*); Alderney aero beacon (*383kHz, 'ALD', 50M, cont.*); Cherbourg Fort de l'Ouest (*312.6kHz, 'RB', 20M, Nos. 2, 4, 6 with Nab Tower*); Pointe de Barfleur (*291.9kHz, 'FG', 70M, No. 6*).

Weather Forecasts (all times GMT except where otherwise stated)

BBC shipping forecast areas:

   Wight, Portland

VHF coast radio stations:

   Niton—0833, 2003, on Ch. 28

   Cherbourg—0633, 1133, on Ch. 27

Marinecall:

   Tel. 0898 500 457

Local radio coastal forecasts:

   BBC Radio Solent—Mon–Fri at local time 0745; Sat at 0730, 0835, 1259, 1402, 1533, 1925; Sun at 0835, 0850, 0930, 1030, 1304, 1504. Frequencies: *999 and 1359 kHz, 221 and 300m, 96.1 MHz FM*

Met Office forecasts:

   Southampton Weather Centre, Tel. 0703 228844

6 POOLE TO ALDERNEY

The passage from Poole to Alderney is one of the shortest crossings in the middle part of the English Channel. From Poole fairway buoy to Alderney's Braye harbour is 57 miles, about 8 miles less then from Yarmouth, Isle of Wight, to Cherbourg's Fort de l'Ouest. The direct course from just off Handfast Point to Braye is approximately 192°T.

The two main hazards are provided by shipping and by the relatively strong tidal streams. You can expect steady and sometimes heavy traffic across the S half of the passage, ploughing its way between the Casquets and Dover Straits separation schemes. To keep the navigator on his toes, the cross-tides off the N side of Alderney can reach 4 knots at springs, and even 10 miles or so S of St Alban's Head you can experience 3–3½ knots at the height of the W-going stream.

A due westerly or easterly will give you an efficient reach either way across the Channel, although for part of the passage the wind will be blowing directly against the tide, which will tend to steepen the seas. A south-westerly makes Alderney hard to lay on the way out, but gives you a free run on the way back. A settled north-westerly is good for either direction, providing a quartering wind for going outward yet not too tight a slant for the return trip.

Alderney, as well as being an attractive and friendly port-of-call in its own right, serves as a convenient staging post for south coast yachts bound for any of the other Channel Islands or for North Brittany. Given reasonable weather, you can cover Poole to Braye harbour in a longish day, have a good night's rest, and then contemplate a more relaxing trip down to Guernsey, or even Jersey, the following day. Thereafter, Guernsey to Lézardrieux or Jersey to St Malo are both pleasant day sails under the right conditions.

Braye, Alderney's only harbour, lies on the N side of the island and is open to the NE. The landfall from this direction is fairly straightforward in good visibility, but the strengthening tides in the final approaches make it necessary to keep an accurate running plot of your position.

Close to the E of Braye entrance are the various drying rocks which border the NE tip of Alderney and extend offshore for just over ¼ mile. In poor visibility, it is important not to make a landfall in the vicinity of these dangers. A couple of miles W of Braye is the grass-capped islet of Burhou, from which drying ledges extend northwards for up to 6 cables and westwards for nearly 1½ miles. Between Burhou and Alderney is the channel known as The

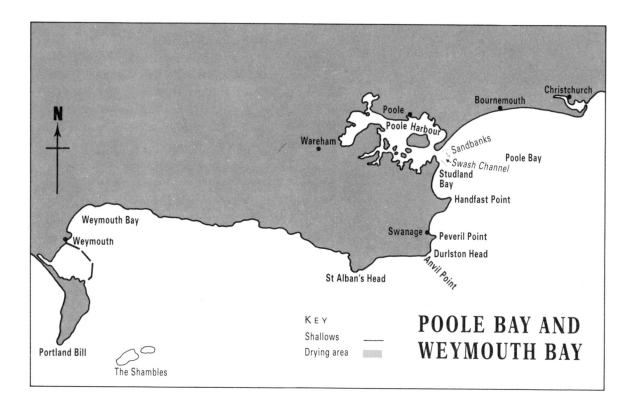

N

Christchurch

Bournemouth

Poole
Poole Harbour

Wareham

Sandbanks
Swash Channel
Poole Bay
Studland
Bay

Handfast Point

Weymouth Bay

Weymouth

Swanage   Peveril Point
Durlston Head
Anvil Point

St Alban's Head

KEY
Shallows   ——
Drying area

POOLE BAY AND
WEYMOUTH BAY

Portland Bill

The Shambles

Swinge, less than ¾ mile wide and notorious for its strong tidal streams and steep overfalls.

The passage from Poole harbour leads you out through the Swash Channel to Poole fairway buoy, SE for about 1 mile to clear the overfalls off Handfast Point, then S by W and seawards past Peveril Point, Durlston Head and Anvil Point. The timing of your departure is not too critical, although it is preferable to carry an outgoing tide past Brownsea Castle and through the narrows between Sandbanks and South Haven Point.

The most common strategy is simply to aim to make the crossing during daylight and therefore to leave Poole as soon as convenient after the 0555 shipping forecast, the 0603 weather forecast, and an early breakfast. Assuming you can lay the course, the 57 miles from Poole fairway to Braye

will take about 12 hours at 5 knots, say from 0730 to 1930. If you expect to make a slower average speed, you ought to leave a bit earlier.

You can enter Braye at any state of tide, so the time of high water, of itself, has no bearing on this aspect of the passage planning. If possible, though, there is much to be said for making the final approach to Alderney near slack water, either 5-6 hours after or 1-2 hours before HW Dover. For a first visit, it is also preferable to avoid spring tides, both for this landfall and for any planned passage on to Guernsey or Jersey in the next day or two. These factors, taken together, point to a dead neap period when HW Dover is around 1930 GMT and LW Poole is near midday.

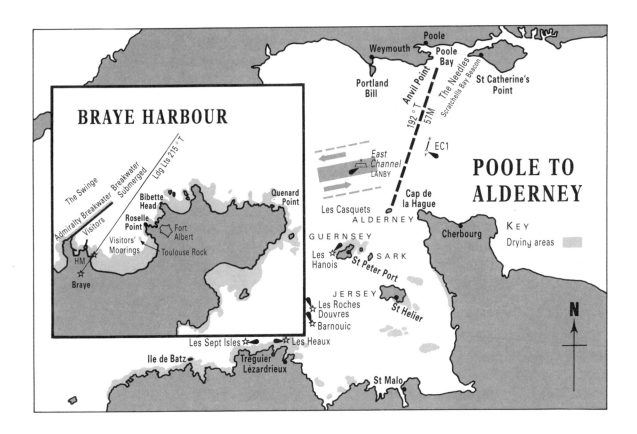

Setting the Course

Assuming that wind and weather will allow you to make directly towards Alderney, it is worth doing some careful homework on your best 'course to steer'. Decide on a realistic time for leaving your berth in Poole and then work out a passage departure time from, say, a position about 1½ miles due E of Durlston Head.

At an average speed of 5 knots, it is just over 10 hours from this point of departure to Braye harbour entrance; at 4 knots, it is nearer 13 hours. Plot the estimated number of hourly tidal vectors as accurately as you can. I find *Stanford's Tidal Atlas* of greater help here than the *Admiralty Atlas*, because not only are directions and rates of streams easy to

interpolate across the lines of flow, but there is also a useful table for interpolating between springs and neaps.

As you draw away from the Dorset coast, you can check your set and drift with visual bearings on St Alban's Head, Anvil Point and, in clear visibility, Portland Bill. The distant Needles or St Catherine's Point can also be useful. As the land sinks hull-down and you approach mid-Channel, Portland Bill and St Catherine's RDF beacons will give you a good angle of cut and can provide some indication of whether you are experiencing the tidal streams as predicted; at 25–35 miles range, though, it is not always easy to get a fine null.

If, for this crossing, you do manage to select a period of neap tides where HW Dover falls around

0700 and 1930 GMT, you will experience a broadly W-going stream for the first half of the trip and an E-going stream for the second half. Therefore, by the time you reach mid-Channel, you may have been set to within 8 or 9 miles of the East Channel light-float—but probably not close enough to be able to spot it by day, let alone identify it with any certainty.

On the other hand, if you cannot avoid making the passage during springs, and the first 5 hours of tide set you powerfully eastwards, then you may at least have the advantage of passing quite close to the East Channel buoy EC1, which lies about 22 miles NNE of Cap de la Hague. This will enable you to fix your position with some confidence and you can then, if necessary, update your course to steer for the 'last leg'.

As you approach Alderney, the island's powerful aero beacon (383kHz, 'ALD', 50M, cont.) will provide a useful position line. In hazy weather, you can usefully cross this with the Casquets beacon (298.8kHz, 'QS', 50M, No. 3), and obtain a reasonable cut when you are between 5 and 10 miles out. Approaching Alderney at night, you can obtain a good set of cross-bearings from the lights on the Casquets (Fl5, 30s, 28M), Quenard Point (Fl4, 15s, 28M), and Cap de la Hague (Fl, 5s, 22M).

Poor Visibility

It is not prudent to approach Alderney in very poor visibility, except perhaps with the aid of a well-tried and trusted Decca set. However, so long as you can see at least 1 mile, it is possible to home in on Braye harbour using Alderney aero beacon. Within a few miles' range you will obtain a very sharp null, and a bearing of 198°T leads you safely in from seaward towards Braye.

If fog looks at all likely once you have committed yourself to the cross-Channel passage, the safest course of action is to break off and make for Cherbourg instead. Although you still have strongish cross-tides between Cap de la Hague and Pointe de Barfleur, at least the coast is relatively clear of dangers on the Cap de la Hague side. Try and make for the Cherbourg Approaches CH1 whistle buoy, and then home in on the W entrance using the low-range RDF beacon which transmits from Fort de l'Ouest lighthouse (312.6kHz, 'RB', 20M, Nos. 2, 4, 6).

Bad Weather

If, while you are on passage between Poole and Alderney, a westerly or north-westerly backs into the SW and freshens, you can always bear away for Cherbourg. Safe of access in all weathers, Cherbourg is almost a copy-book port of refuge, and you will start to obtain shelter from a strong south-westerly as you begin to close the land to the E of Cap de la Hague.

Fresh easterly weather is not recommended for a first visit to Alderney. Not only does the Channel always seem particularly lumpy with even a moderate easterly blowing, but a strengthening wind from this quarter can make Cherbourg difficult to reach if you decide to alter course late in the passage. Braye harbour is open to the NE and should be avoided in all but very light winds from this direction.

The Return Passage

As with the outward passage, most yachtsmen contemplating the return trip from Alderney to Poole plan to leave Braye early in the morning and complete the crossing before nightfall. Even if you don't follow this schedule exactly, it is at least advisable to make the first part of the passage in daylight, when you are crossing the busy shipping lanes.

Once you are past the down-Channel lanes, the RDF beacons at Portland and St Catherine's should give a good cut and add further data to your EP. As you approach the coast, you can also try the two VHF beacons at Anvil Point and Scratchells Bay. These directional transmitters alternate on VHF Ch. 88 and have a nominal range of 14 and 30 miles respectively. You have to identify the station, wait for a starting signal, and count the number of beats until a 'null' in the transmission. A table in the Almanac will then give the station's bearing from seaward.

When planning this landfall, and depending on how the tides work out, I usually aim for a position well out into Poole Bay, rather than make directly for Anvil Point, risk being set towards St Alban's race, and then have to slog back against a W-going stream. This strategy can pay off in poor visibility, when you don't really want to tangle with the strong streams and various patches of overfalls between St Alban's Head and Handfast Point.

Poor Visibility

By closing the land in Poole Bay itself, you not only stay in uncomplicated water, but the soundings also give a gradual indication of your progress shorewards. As you draw N of Anvil Point, you should be able to pick up Hurn aero beacon (*322kHz, 'HRN', 15M, cont.*). Although this is located 5 miles inland, it can give reasonable results when bearing roughly perpendicular to the coast. In the outer approaches to Poole Bay, a position line from Hurn can be crossed with Anvil Point VHF beacon; closer inshore, Scratchells Bay beacon gives a more accurate cut.

For the final approach to Poole harbour entrance in murky weather, you can obtain some help from the low-range beacon which transmits from North Haven Point on Sandbanks (*303.4kHz, 'PO', 10M, Nos. 3 and 6*). Once you have located Poole fairway buoy, which has a bell, you can either pick your way carefully up the Swash Channel, or else sound into Studland Bay and anchor.

High-speed Factors

The 57 miles from Poole fairway buoy to Braye harbour entrance will take about 4 hours at 15 knots, or only 3 hours at 20 knots. You can therefore arrive in time for lunch by making a reasonably early start, but it is particularly important to do your tidal homework for this passage. You need to make an accurate landfall on Alderney and, even in 3 or 4 hours, the tidal set E or W can easily be 10 miles, depending on which part of the cycle you hit and whether the tides are springs or neaps.

It is preferable to arrive off Alderney near slack water, either 5–6 hours after or 1–2 hours before HW Dover. This would mean clearing Poole fairway buoy something like 2 hours after or 5 hours before HW Dover. In the first case you'd have mostly W-going tide on the passage, and in the second case it would all be E-going. The first departure time would therefore give you a quieter sea if the wind was anywhere from the E, and the second would be better if the wind was anywhere from the W.

It is worth setting two intermediate decision waypoints along your intended track, one in mid-Channel and one perhaps about 10 miles from Braye. In conjuction with an offshore waypoint 5 miles NNW of Cherbourg's Fort de l'Ouest, it is then straightforward to divert to Cherbourg if you meet freshening weather from the W or SW, or if conditions look like being murky off Alderney.

Alderney tends to show up well on radar, although you will probably pick up the higher, middle part of the island first. English Channel buoy EC1 has a Racon ('T', 90s, 10M), although you will pass it just about on its nominal range if you are more or less on track for Braye. Casquets lighthouse has a more powerful Racon ('T', 25M), which is useful on the approach to Alderney. If you do divert to Cherbourg, the coast between Cap de la Hague and Cherbourg is a good radar target.

Pilot Books, etc.

Admiralty NP27, *The Channel Pilot*.

Admiralty NP74, *List of Lights, Vol. A.*

Channel Harbours and Anchorages, K. Adlard Coles, 6th edn 1985, published by Nautical.

Channel Island Pilot, M. Robson, 4th edn 1990, published by Nautical.

The Shell Pilot to the English Channel, J. Coote, vols 1 and 2, 1987 edns, published by Faber and Faber.

Channel Islands and North Brittany Cruising, P. Cumberlidge, 1st edn 1990, published by Yachting Monthly.

The Cruising Association Handbook, 7th edn 1990, published by the Cruising Association.

Charts

Admiralty:

No. 2675—The English Channel

No. 2615—Bill of Portland to the Needles

No. 2175—Poole Bay

No. 2611—Poole Harbour and Approaches

No. 3653—Guernsey to Alderney and adjacent coast of France

No. 60—Alderney and the Casquets

No. 2845—Alderney Harbour

No. 1106—Approaches to Cherbourg

Imray:

C4—Needles to Portland

C10—Western English Channel Passage Chart

C33A—Channel Islands, North

Y23—Poole Harbour

Stanford:

No. 7—English Channel, Central Section

No. 15—Poole and Christchurch Harbours

No. 16—The Channel Islands

Tidal Atlases

Stanford's Tidal Atlas, English Channel West (recommended).

Admiralty NP250, *English and Bristol Channels.*

Tidal Streams (times based on HW Dover)

Position	E-going stream starts	W-going stream starts
5 miles S of Anvil Point	+0530	−0030
10 miles NNE of Braye harbour	+0550	−0040
Just off Braye harbour	+0520	−0145

Tidal Differences and Heights

Place	Time of HW on Dover	Heights above chart datum in metres			
		MHWS	MLWS	MHWN	MLWN
Poole harbour (entrance)	–	2.0, 1.5	0.3	1.4, 1.6	1.1
Poole Bridge	–	2.2, 1.7	0.4	1.5, 1.8	1.0
Braye harbour	−0405	6.3	0.8	4.7	2.6

Important Lights

English coast:
Anvil Point (*Fl, 10s, 24M, vis 237°–076°T*); Portland Bill (*Fl4, 20s, 29M; FR, 13M, vis 271°–291°T*); St Catherine's Point (*Fl, 5s, 30M, vis 257°–117°T; FR, 17M, vis 099°–116°T*); the Needles (*Oc2, 20s, WRG, 17M, 14M, 14M*); Swanage pierhead light (*2FRvert, 3M*); Poole fairway buoy (*LFl, 10s, bell*); Training Bank beacon (*QR, 2M*).

Alderney landfall:
Quenard Point (*Fl4, 15s, 28M, vis 085°–027°T*); the Casquets (*Fl5, 30s, 28M*); Cap de la Hague (*Fl, 5s, 22M*); Château à l'Etoc Point (*IsoWR, 4s, 10M, 7M*); Braye harbour leading lights in line 215°T—*front at the old pier (QFl, 17M, intens 210°–220°T), rear (Iso, 10s, 18M, intens 210°–220°T*).

RDF Beacons

English coast:
Portland Bill (*291.9kHz, 'PB', 50M, No. 1*); St Catherine's Point (*291.9kHz, 'CP', 50M, No. 2*); Hurn aero beacon (*322kHz, 'HRN', 15M, cont.*); Poole harbour, Sandbanks beacon (*303.4kHz, 'PO', 10M, Nos. 3 and 6*); Anvil Point VHF beacon (*VHF Ch. 88, 'AL', 14M, alt with 'HD'*); High Down Scratchells Bay VHF beacon (*VHF Ch. 88, 'HD', 30M, alt with 'AL'*).

Alderney landfall:
Alderney aero beacon (*383kHz, 'ALD', 50M, cont.*); Casquets lighthouse (*298.8kHz, 'QS', 50M, No. 3*).

Weather Forecasts (all times GMT except where otherwise stated)

BBC shipping forecast area:
Portland

VHF coast radio stations:
Niton —0833, 2003, on Ch. 28
Weymouth Bay—0833, 2003, on Ch. 5
Cherbourg—0633, 1133, on Ch. 27
Jersey Radio—0645, 0745, 1245, 1845, 2245, on Chs 25 and 82

Marinecall:
Tel. 0898 500 457. Also British Telecom service for Channel Islands area, Tel. 0481 64033

Local radio coastal forecasts:
ILR Bournemouth (Two Counties Radio)—sea conditions report every day at local times 0708, 0808, 0908, 1306, 1700; inshore shipping forecast on Fri at local time 1708, Sat at 0750 and 1310, Sun at 0830. Frequencies: *828 kHz, 362m, 97.2 MHz FM*

Met Office forecasts:
Southampton Weather Centre, Tel. 0703 228844

7 CHERBOURG TO THE CHANNEL ISLANDS

Chapter 5 looked at one of the most popular of English Channel crossings, the 60-mile passage from the Needles to Cherbourg. In this passage we take a break from the open sea and continue W and S from Cherbourg towards the Channel Islands, a coasting leg which forms the second stage of many a summer cruise to Brittany and beyond.

From Cherbourg W entrance to Guernsey's St Peter Port is an interesting day sail of about 42 miles, which usually takes even a smallish boat no more than 6 hours, working your tides and given the right weather. You have the option of making two hops and stopping over at Braye harbour, Alderney. Having reached St Peter Port, you are well placed to visit the nearby islands of Herm and Sark, to head SE for Jersey, Granville, Chausey or St Malo, or else to carry on farther S and W for the North Brittany harbours of Paimpol, Lézardrieux or Tréguier.

Between Cherbourg and St Peter Port, however, there are two potentially tricky tidal 'gateways' to negotiate: the Alderney Race, with its powerful local streams and notorious patches of overfalls; and the Little Russel, that uneasy rock-fringed channel separating Herm from the NE corner of Guernsey. Both stretches of water are rough going in wind-over-tide conditions, especially on a weather-going spring, and a passage through either needs to be planned with care.

When bound S through the Alderney Race, the best time to arrive at a position 2 miles NW of Cap de la Hague is ½ hour *before* HW Dover (or about 4½ hours *after* HW St Helier). It is then slack water in the Race, but the SW-going stream will be just about to start in your favour. From Cherbourg W entrance to this waypoint is 14 miles and so, with a 5-knot cruising speed, you should take your departure 3½ hours before HW Dover (1½ hours after HW St Helier), leaving the marina ½ hour before that.

Now at 3½ hours before HW Dover, the main English Channel stream is still E-going, and will be for the next 3 hours. However, a W-going eddy runs close inshore between Cherbourg and Cap de la Hague, starting about 3 hours before HW Dover off Cherbourg and much earlier farther W. It is important to use this favourable current rather than wait for the main ebb, because otherwise: (a) you will arrive in the Alderney Race when the stream is at its strongest and the overfalls at their most boisterous, and (b) you will not reach Guernsey before the tide turns foul again in the Little Russel.

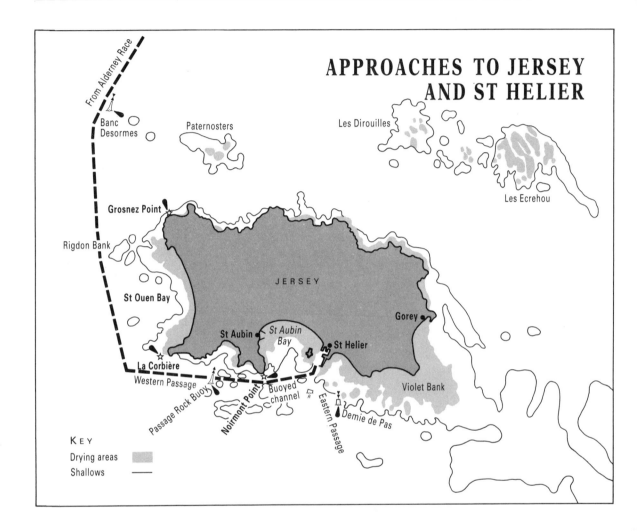

APPROACHES TO JERSEY AND ST HELIER

KEY
Drying areas
Shallows

In westerly weather it may be preferable to leave Cherbourg even earlier than 3½ hours before HW Dover, to allow for working to windward and so as to arrive in the Race while the stream is still trickling N; this will help minimize your exposure to the most critical wind-over-tide conditions.

From Cherbourg's Fort de l'Ouest, head fairly close along the coast towards Pointe de Jardeheu— a track of 292°T for 8½ miles takes you to Basse Bréfort N-cardinal buoy, which marks the end of a rocky ledge extending ¾ mile N of Jardeheu. About

3½ miles along this line you will leave Bannes Rocks N-cardinal beacon tower ½ mile to the S. This beacon stands at the NE corner of quite a wide plateau of shoals and so, when tacking westwards, you should not stand in within a mile of the shore until the Bannes beacon is itself 1 mile E of your own longitude. Once up with the Basse Bréfort buoy, make good 288°T for 4 miles to a position about 1¾ miles N of the tall Gros du Raz lighthouse; this course should leave the smaller La Plate light-tower a good ½ mile to the S.

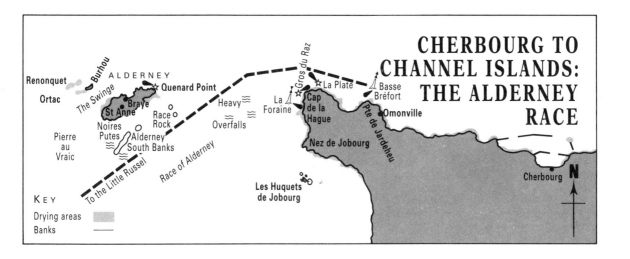

Now alter course to just S of W, steering, if you can see it, for Quenard Point at the NE tip of Alderney. Assuming you have arrived at the best time of tide, that is, ½ hour before HW Dover, the trick is actually to head towards Quenard Point, but then allow the first of the SW-going stream to suck you into the Race. This strategy should allow you to pass well to the N of a sometimes heavy patch of overfalls lying about 3½–4 miles W by S from Gros du Raz. The best line through the Race usually lies from 2–2½ miles S of, and roughly parallel with, the S coast of Alderney. Another heavy area of overfalls often builds up over Alderney South Banks, which this track should leave 1 mile or so to the N.

Approach to the Little Russel

At springs, and following the line just described, the SW-going stream will accelerate you through the Race and past the S coast of Alderney at anything from 2½ to about 6 knots, depending on how long after slack water you make the passage. Peak spring rates in the Race can reach 8 knots, near a position

3 miles W of Cap de la Hague and around 3 hours after HW Dover.

Once you are clear of Alderney, the tide will continue to help you towards Guernsey at up to 3½ knots at springs, the best of the stream being from 1 to 3½ hours after HW Dover. So if you have slipped past Quenard Point at about ¾ hour after HW Dover and maintained your cruising speed of 5 knots, you can expect to be approaching the Little Russel channel only 2 hours later at springs, perhaps 2½ hours at neaps.

The Little Russel lies between the NE tip of Guernsey and the 3-mile stretch of drying rocks which string out NE from the N end of Herm. The most northerly of these dangers are unmarked — Platte Boue (dries 1.8 m) and Boufresse (dries 3.4 m). Platte Boue, the outer of these two, lies ¾ mile NNW of Grande Amfroque (17 m high), a small islet which in turn lies just over 2 miles NE of Herm. Grande Amfroque has two beacons built on it, one white and one black-and-white; their transit leads across Platte Boue as a danger line, bearing about 151 °T from seaward.

On the Guernsey side of the Little Russel, Platte

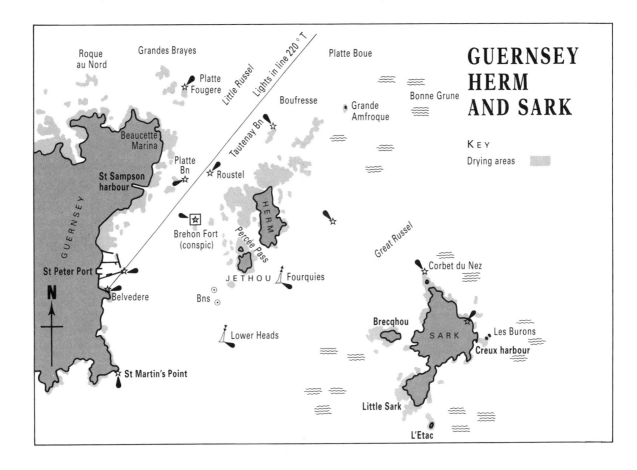

Fougère lighthouse lies not quite 1 mile NE of Fort Doyle, the island's NE tip. When approaching the Little Russel from the direction of Alderney, it is best to hold a track which heads towards Platte Fougère on about 230°T. This line clears Platte Boue by a good 1¼ miles and makes for a safer landfall than that provided by the Herm side of the Russel. Platte Fougère is conspicuous from seaward in good visibility, white with a black horizontal stripe.

When you are about 1½ miles NE of Platte Fougère, steer SSW into the Little Russel, keeping Roustel black-and-white chequered beacon tower in line with Bréhon fort behind it, bearing 198°T.

When a couple of cables from Roustel, make good 220°T to leave Roustel a cable to port, the Platte beacon 2 cables to starboard, and Bréhon fort not quite ½ mile to port. Then make for Castle Cornet and St Peter Port S breakwater.

Having followed the above directions, and of course weather permitting, you should be arriving off St Peter Port between 3 and 4 hours after HW Dover, just as the S-going tide between Guernsey and Herm is starting to ease off. This will be at about 4 hours *before* HW St Peter Port, so you might have an hour or two to wait in the outer harbour before you can safely cross the sill into Victoria Marina.

Guernsey's Beaucette Marina

Built in the early 1970s by blasting a narrow channel from a disused quarry to the sea, this fascinating haven lies close S of Fort Doyle. From the N, leave Platte Fougère ¼ mile to the W and continue due S until you can identify Petite Canupe S-cardinal spar buoy, not quite ¾ mile S of the lighthouse. Leave Petite Canupe close to the N and pick up the Beaucette leading marks: *front*, a red vertical stripe on a white background on the N head of the entrance; *rear*, a similar red stripe on top of a white-painted clubhouse. Keep these in transit bearing 276°T and pass between two pairs of small lateral buoys. The narrow entrance dog-legs to port, leaving a 'tyre' breakwater and a small green buoy to starboard. The visitors' berths are on the S side of the basin. Beaucette makes an interesting alternative to St Peter Port and is accessible 2½–3 hours either side of HW, but do not attempt to enter in fresh E or NE winds.

Direct to Jersey?

Most yachts bound for the Channel Islands from Cherbourg head for Guernsey first, either in one hop or via Alderney. But if your cruising plans include Granville, Iles Chausey or St Malo, there is much to be said for making directly from the Alderney Race to Jersey's St Helier Marina. From here it is an easy day's sail to anywhere in the Gulf of St Malo, and the passages to the French coast are generally more sheltered than those made from Guernsey.

The best timing from Cherbourg through the Alderney Race is the same as for the passage to St Peter Port, but the line through the Race is different. Weather permitting, and having reached a position about 1¾ miles due N of Gros du Raz lighthouse ½ hour before HW Dover, skirt round Cap de la Hague about this distance off, setting off due S along the Cotentin Peninsula to leave Gros du Raz and La Foraine beacon tower to port.

Once abreast Nez de Jobourg and clear of the temperamental areas of the Race, you should set a course for the NW corner of Jersey; from a position 2 miles W of Nez de Jobourg, make good 209°T for 25 miles down to the Banc Desormes W-cardinal buoy, which lies 4 miles NNW of Grosnez Point. This track leaves Blanchard E-cardinal buoy 3 miles to starboard and Sark itself 5 miles to starboard. When approaching the vicinity of Banc Desormes, be sure you are well clear of the Paternosters, a nasty ledge of drying rocks 2–3 miles NE of Grosnez Point.

Coming down the W coast of Jersey, keep outside Rigdon Bank and a good mile W of Corbière lighthouse. There are drying rocks up to ½ mile W and NW of Corbière, so don't turn along Jersey's S coast until Noirmont Point light-tower bears less than 097°T. The W approach to St Helier is straightforward and well buoyed. By keeping up 5 knots from the Alderney Race, you should carry a fair tide all the way to St Helier, arriving near HW.

The two most unwelcome complications on a passage from Cherbourg to the islands are (a) deteriorating visibility, and (b) a freshening W or SW wind which will kick up a steep sea in a SW-going tide, especially in the Alderney Race and Little Russel.

Poor Visibility

In patchy visibility you can usually find your way along to Cap de la Hague and slip through the Race, but you are then left with the problem of keeping an accurate EP in the strong and rather unpredictable streams. Without the assistance of Decca or radar, a landfall on the Little Russel is a nightmare in murky weather—on one side you have the long tail of drying dangers extending NE from Herm; on the other, there are extensive rocks to the S and W of Platte Fougère.

It is advisable to stay in Cherbourg and have a good lunch if the visibility looks dubious, but if the weather closes in as you reach the Alderney Race, it is usually preferable to hold well to the N of Quenard Point and make for Braye harbour, rather than carry on for St Peter Port. If you can't easily reach Braye or return to Cherbourg, Jersey is a much safer bet than Guernsey in mist or fog. A back-bearing of the Alderney RDF beacon should keep you clear of the Paternosters, while Corbière and Jersey West beacons will help the passage westabout the island.

Once round Corbière and its off-lying rocks, it is feasible, using RDF and its foghorn (*Mo'C', 60s*), to home in close to the lighthouse *from the S* and then edge your way along the S coast of Jersey into St Aubin Bay, especially with the tide high and falling slack.

Freshening Winds

If possible, pick some quiet weather for a first passage through the Alderney Race and the Little Russel. Even a moderate south-westerly against a fresh spring tide will make for hard sailing when you are trying to concentrate on marks and bearings. If, however, you are through the Race and the wind draws ahead and freshens, you can either bear away for Jersey or continue towards Guernsey via the Great Russel, between Herm and Sark.

The Great Russel is much wider than the Little Russel and is relatively steep-to on the Sark (E) side. There are still heavy overfalls on a weather-going tide, but the pilotage is simpler and there is more room to manoeuvre. Once you are S of Herm and abreast of Brecqhou, pass S of the Lower Heads S-cardinal buoy and head NW for St Peter Port. In quiet conditions, good visibility and above half-tide, there is a route to St Peter Port between Herm and Jethou, by way of the Percée Pass and Alligande Pass. When making for the Great Russel from the Alderney Race, pass N and W of the often turbulent Banc de la Schôle, which lies about half-way between the two.

High-speed Factors

The 42-mile coastal passage from Cherbourg to Guernsey can make a pleasant morning or afternoon run, depending on the tides. It can also be a very unpleasant trip if conditions are boisterous in the Alderney Race or the Little Russel. It is just as important for high-speed motor-boats to time their passage carefully as it is for yachts, not so much because of having the tide fair or foul (although this can be significant with rates sometimes in excess of 6 or 7 knots) but mainly because of sea-state.

The copy-book strategy is to arrive off the Alderney Race at dead slack water, just as the SW-going stream is about to turn in your favour. For this you need to time your departure from Cherbourg in order to arrive at a waypoint 2 miles NW of Cap de la Hague ½ hour before HW Dover (or about 4½ hours after HW St Helier). You can reckon on 14 miles from Cherbourg's Fort de l'Ouest to this waypoint, just under 1 hour at 15 knots

or ¾ hour at 20 knots.

From Cap de la Hague, head towards Quenard Point for a couple of miles before turning to the SW. The best line through the Race usually lies 2–2½ miles S of and roughly parallel with the S coast of Alderney. Thereafter, follow the directions for Guernsey given in this chapter, making for a 'lining-up' waypoint 3 miles NE of Platte Fougère lighthouse and then entering the Little Russel by heading for a waypoint 1 cable due west of Roustel tower.

Platte Fougère has a Racon beacon, but you must use radar with care if the visibility is poor. The coast between Cherbourg and Cap de la Hague shows up well, as does the S coast of Alderney, but the NE end of Guernsey is very low-lying and tends to be elusive on the screen. You usually pick up the higher ground towards the S side of Guernsey first, so be careful not to jump to dangerous conclusions about your distance off.

In murky visibility, or if the wind is southerly and your experience of the

Alderney Race suggests that the Little Russel might be nasty, you can opt for the Great Russel between Herm and Sark before approaching St Peter Port from the S. This route involves only a slight increase in passage time for a fast motor-boat. Although the Great Russel can serve up heavy overfalls on a weather-going tide, the seas are not as steep as in the Little Russel, the pilotage is simpler and the channel much wider.

In very poor visibility, Jersey is a safer and easier passage than Guernsey. From the Alderney Race make for Banc Desormes W-cardinal buoy, which lies 4 miles NNW of Jersey's Grosnez Point. Coming down the W coast of Jersey, keep outside Rigdon Bank and a good mile W of Corbière lighthouse before lining up for the Western Passage to St Helier. The island shows up well on radar. There is a useful Racon beacon on the Western Passage leading line, but don't confuse it with the Demie de Pas Racon.

Pilot Books, etc.

Admiralty NP27, *The Channel Pilot*.

Admiralty NP74, *List of Lights, Vol. A*.

Channel Harbours and Anchorages, K. Adlard Coles, 6th edn 1985, published by Nautical.

The Shell Pilot to the English Channel, J. Coote, vol. 2, 1987 edn, published by Faber and Faber.

The Cruising Association Handbook, 7th edn 1990, published by the Cruising Association.

Channel Island Pilot, M. Robson, 4th edn 1990, published by Nautical.

Normandy and Channel Island Pilot. M. Brackenbury, 7th edn (revised) 1990, published by Adlard Coles.

Channel Islands and North Brittany Cruising, P. Cumberlidge, 1st edn 1990, published by Yachting Monthly.

Adlard Coles Pilot Pack, Vol. 3, B. Goulder, 1st edn 1989, published by Adlard Coles.

Charts

Admiralty:

No. 2669—The Channel Islands and adjacent coast of France

No. 1106—Approaches to Cherbourg

No. 2602—Cherbourg

No. 3653—Guernsey to Alderney and adjacent coast of France

No. 60—Alderney and the Casquets

No. 808—East Guernsey, Herm and Sark

Imray:

C33A—Channel Islands, North

Stanford:

No. 16—The Channel Islands

Tidal Atlases

Stanford's Tidal Atlas, English Channel West.

Admiralty NP264, *The Channel Islands and adjacent coast of France*.

Tidal Streams (times based on HW Dover)

Position	E-going stream starts	W-going stream starts
Close off Cherbourg	+0500	−0230
Close N of Basse Bréfort buoy	+0515	−0500
Alderney Race, midway between Quenard Point and Gros du Raz	+0540	−0030
The Swinge	+0530	−0030
Jersey, S coast close inshore	+0230	−0400

Position	N-going stream starts	S-going stream starts
Little Russel, N end	+0500	−0120
Jersey, 2 miles W of Grosnez Point	−0450	+0120

Tidal Differences and Heights

Place	Time of HW on Dover	Heights above chart datum in metres			
		MHWS	MLWS	MHWN	MLWN
Cherbourg	−0340	6.2	0.8	4.8	2.3
Omonville	−0350	6.1	0.8	4.7	2.4
Braye harbour	−0405	6.3	0.8	4.7	2.6
St Peter Port	−0440	9.0	1.0	6.7	3.5
St Helier	−0450	11.1	1.3	8.1	4.1

Note: Victoria Marina, St Peter Port, is accessible for about 2½ hours either side of local HW for, say, 1.5 m draft.
St Helier Marina is accessible for 3 hours either side of local HW for any draft up to 2 m.

Important Lights

Cherbourg to Alderney:

Cherbourg Fort de l'Ouest (*Fl3, WR, 15s, 23M, 19M; W vis 122°-355°T, R vis 355°-122°T*); Cherbourg Fort de l'Est (*IsoWG, 4s, 10M, 6M; W vis 008°-229°T, R vis 229°-008°T*); Cap de la Hague, Rocher Gros du Raz (*Fl, 5s, 24M, vis 354°-274°T*); Cap de la Hague, La Plate (*Fl, 2+1, WR, 12s, 9M, 6M; W vis 115°-272°T, R vis 272°-115°T*); Quenard Point (*Fl4, 15s, 28M, vis 085°-027°T*); The Casquets (*Fl5, 30s, 28M*); Château à l'Étoc Point (*IsoWR, 4s, 10M, 7M*); Braye harbour leading lights in line 215°T (*both intens 210°-220°T*)—front at the old pier (*QFl, 17M*), rear (*Iso, 10s, 18M*).

Little Russel and Guernsey:

Platte Fougère lighthouse (*LFl, WR, 10s, 16M; W vis 155°-085°T, R vis 085°-155°T*); Tautenay beacon (*Q3WR, 6s, 7M; W vis 050°-215°T, R vis 215°-050°T*); Roustel tower (*QFl, 7M*); Platte beacon (*Fl, 3s, WR, 7M, 5M; W vis 219°-024°T, R vis 024°-219°T*); Bréhon fort (*Iso, 4s, 9M*); St Peter Port leading lights in line 220°T—front Castle Breakwater head (*Alt. WR, 10s, 16M, vis 187°-007°T*), rear Belvedere (*Oc10s, 14M, vis 179°-269°T*); White Rock pierhead (*OcG, 5s, 14M, intens 174°-354°T*); St Martin's Point, SE tip of Guernsey (*Fl3, WR, 10s, 14M; R vis 185°-191°T, W vis 191°-011°T, R vis 011°-081°T*); Les Hanois, lighthouse off the SW tip of Guernsey (*Q2, 5s, 23M, vis 294°-237°T*).

Great Russel and Sark:

Noire Pute Rock, 1 mile E of Herm, has a light whose red sector covers all the dangers on the W side of the Great Russel from Bonne Grune to the Lower Heads buoy (*Fl2, WR, 15s, 6M; R vis 040°-220°T, W vis 220°-040°T*); Sark, Corbet du Nez (*Fl4, WR, 15s, 8M; W vis 057°-230°T, R vis 230°-057°T*); Sark, Point Robert (*Fl, 15s, 28M*); Fourquies Rock N-cardinal buoy, 7 cables E by S of Jethou (*QFl*); Lower Heads S-cardinal buoy (*Q6+LFl, 15s*).

W coast of Jersey and W approaches to St Helier:

Grosnez Point (*Fl2, WR, 15s, 19M, 17M; W vis 081°-188°T, R vis 188°-241°T, obscured elsewhere*); Banc Desormes W-cardinal buoy (*Q9, 15s*); La Corbière (*Iso, WR, 10s, 17M, 16M; W vis shore-294°T, R vis 294°-328°T, W vis 328°-148°T, R vis 148°T-shore*); Noirmont Point (*Fl4, 12s, 13M*); Western Passage leading lights in line 082°T—front La Grève d'Azette (*Oc5s, 14M, vis 034°-129°T*), rear Mont Ubé (*Alt. WR, 6s, 12M, vis 250°-095°T*); Platte lattice beacon (*FlR, 1½s, 5M*); St Helier (Small Roads) leading lights in line 023°T, synchronized—front Albert Pier elbow (*OcG, 5s, 11M*), rear Esplanade (*OcR, 5s, 12M*).

RDF Beacons

Cherbourg Fort de l'Ouest (*312.6kHz, 'RB', 20M, Nos. 2, 4, 6, with Nab Tower*); Alderney aero beacon (*383kHz, 'ALD', 50M, cont.*); Casquets lighthouse (*298.8kHz, 'QS', 50M, No. 3*); Guernsey aero beacon (*361kHz, 'GUR', 30M, cont.*); St Peter Port, Castle breakwater (*285kHz, 'GY', 10M, cont.*); Jersey West aero beacon (*329kHz, 'JW', 25M, cont.*); La Corbière (*305.7kHz, 'CB', 20M, Nos. 2, 4, 6*); St Helier approaches, Elizabeth Castle (*287.3kHz, 'EC', 10M, cont.*).

Weather Forecasts (all times GMT except where otherwise stated)

BBC shipping forecast areas:

Wight, Portland

VHF coast radio stations:

Cherbourg—0633, 1133, on Ch. 27

Jersey Radio—0645, 0745, 1245, 1845, 2245, on Chs 25 and 82

Recorded telephone forecast:

Tel. 0481 64033

Met Office forecasts:

Jersey Airport Met Office, Tel. 0534 23660 or 46111

8 THE CHANNEL ISLANDS TO BRITTANY

Those who undertake a Brittany cruise by way of the Channel Islands often find they begin to relax and feel that their holiday has really started once they've arrived safely at Guernsey's St Peter Port or Jersey's St Helier. From either of these secure and convenient marinas, a fascinating range of cruising lies close to hand, subject to wind, weather and tide, and depending on how far you feel like travelling each day.

If you have the time, it can be very pleasant to spend a week day-sailing from St Peter Port, exploring various anchorages off the nearby islands of Herm and Sark and, indeed, around Guernsey itself. If you are keen to press on for France, there are three useful passages starting from St Peter Port: a short hop SE to Jersey, bringing you within easy reach of Granville, Iles Chausey, Cancale or St Malo; a somewhat longer haul SSE to St Malo direct; or a day passage SW to Lézardrieux or Tréguier. This last option will leave you well placed to continue farther W along the Brittany coast, or to head E for St Malo and thus back to Granville or Chausey.

Many English yachts now make for Jersey straight from Cherbourg, without calling at Guernsey first. From St Helier, the scope for local sailing is not so great as from St Peter Port, but you have the choice of well-marked day passages to Granville, Chausey or St Malo, or a more open leg WSW to Lézardrieux.

St Peter Port to St Helier

From pierhead to pierhead this trip is 25 miles. If you average 5 knots, it is best to leave St Peter Port soon after local LW, which will mean coming out of Victoria marina within a couple of hours of HW and waiting outside in the pool, either alongside the marina holding pontoon or moored to a pair of visitors' buoys.

The main part of the passage, from just outside St Peter Port harbour to a position 1 mile due W of La Corbière lighthouse, involves making good 150°T for 19 miles. The tide will be setting S and then SSW in the first hour, S in the second hour, SSE in the third hour and SE as you approach Corbière. With a fair wind and the more or less favourable stream, you ought to arrive off Corbière within 3½ hours of leaving St Peter Port, and probably a bit earlier at springs. There will then be plenty of fair tide left for the last 6 miles to St Helier. La Corbière RDF beacon is useful in hazy weather (*305.7kHz, 'CB', 20M,*

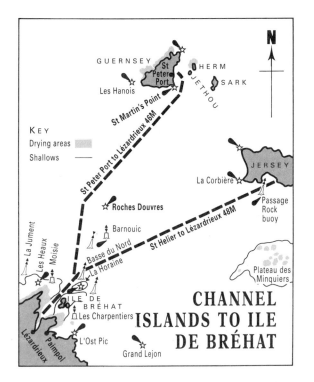

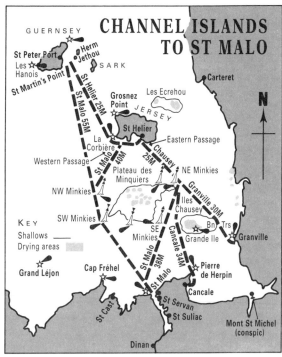

Nos. 2, 4, 6) and can be cut with a bearing from Roches Douvres beacon (*298.8kHz, 'RD', 70M, No. 4*).

The reason for keeping 1 mile off Corbière is to give a wide berth to the various drying rocks which extend W and NW from that headland. However, once Noirmont Point light-tower, 3½miles ESE of Corbière, bears 095°T, you should make good in that direction, allowing at first for the SE-going stream which will be trying to set you southward until you are well E of Corbière.

The Western Passage to St Helier leads 4 cables N of Passage Rock N-cardinal buoy and then between Noirmont Point tower and the Four N-cardinal buoy. From here make good 082° for not quite 2 miles towards the end of Elizabeth breakwater, leaving Raudière green conical buoy close to starboard and two red cans to port. Pass between La

Platte red lattice beacon and East Rock green conical buoy and turn NNE into the Small Roads towards St Helier harbour entrance. There is a low-range RDF beacon on Elizabeth Castle (*287.3kHz, 'EC', 10M, cont.*).

St Peter Port to St Malo Direct

This longish passage of nearly 55 miles takes you 7 miles W of Jersey and then westabout the notorious Plateau des Minquiers, known locally as the Minkies. After 29 miles, you will need to leave the NW Minkies buoy reasonably close to the E, so there is much to be said for setting off from St Peter Port at around 1700 and making the trip overnight. In good visibility, bearings from the powerful lighthouses at La Corbière, Roches Douvres and Cap Fréhel give a good cut near the NW Minkies.

The NW and SW Minkies buoys are just over 5 miles apart and both lit. The direct track from St Peter Port to the SW Minkies buoy leaves the NW Minkies ½ mile to the E. Having reached and identified the SW Minkies buoy, alter to the SE to make good 150°T for 15 miles towards the St Malo fairway buoy.

By opting for an overnight passage, you should be able to identify lights on the French coast as you make your landfall, but the final approach to St Malo can be timed for soon after dawn. The Chenal de la Petite Porte is the natural entrance channel when coming from this direction, but the Chenal de la Grande Porte is useful if you make your landfall much farther W than the St Malo fairway buoy.

Cruising at 5 knots, this passage spans two tides, so your departure time from St Peter Port will probably be determined as much by your schedule as by the streams. However, it is useful to have a S-going run in the Little Russel when you leave, and to have a slack or W-going stream when passing the Minkies. You can achieve these objectives by leaving St Peter Port about 1 hour after local LW, arriving off the NW Minkies near local HW.

St Peter Port to Lézardrieux or Tréguier

A direct line from the SW tip of Guernsey to the outer marks of the Trieux River is something like 35 miles in a south-south-westerly direction. Unfortunately, it is not possible to sail a straight track because the extensive rocky outcrop of Roches Douvres lies right in the way. About 4½ miles S of Roches Douvres is a much smaller patch of drying rocks, Plateau de Barnouic, which has a shallow bank, the Banc du Moulec, a couple of miles to the WNW. The tide runs strongly in the vicinity of all these dangers.

The Roches Douvres stretch about 2 miles from W to E and nearly 1½ miles N to S. The lighthouse is 200 ft high and has a useful RDF beacon (298.8kHz, 'RD', 70M, No. 4). Even in daylight, given reasonable visibility, you can often identify the lighthouse before losing the S coast of Guernsey; summer haze permitting, it should then remain in sight until you pick up those first enigmatic smudges of North Brittany.

My strategy has usually been to pass Roches Douvres down-tide with plenty of room to spare. Coming westabout, I prefer to view the gaunt stone tower from a safe distance of at least 3 miles. In fact, on this passage from St Peter Port to Lézardrieux, I almost always pass westabout Roches Douvres and the plan generally seems to work out as follows:

1 Leave Victoria Marina 2 hours after local HW (a bit earlier at dead neaps) with a safe margin over the sill.

2 Push the foul but slackening tide down to St Martin's Point and set a course to make good towards a position 3–4 miles W of Roches Douvres lighthouse. This leg is 24 miles and the stream will be setting broadly W for the next 4½ hours, with some S in it towards local LW. It is important to make good at least 5 knots so that you are well past Roches Douvres before the new flood starts running E.

3 Now set a course for a position 1 mile NW of Basse du Nord N-cardinal buoy, which marks the N extremity of dangers lurking seaward of La Horaine tower. This track leads right onto the Grand Chenal de Trieux leading line, but it is vital to make adequate allowance for the powerful flood stream, which will be setting ESE across the entrance by the time you arrive. Spring rates here can reach 6 knots locally,

somewhat in excess of the figures given in the tidal atlases. You should keep continual track of progress on your way in, since it is all too easy to be set too far to the E.

The approach to the Trieux can be stressful in murky visibility, but the low-range RDF beacon on Ile de Bréhat is sometimes useful (*294.2kHz, 'DO', 10M, Nos. 1, 5*). When planning this passage, bear in mind that the outer dangers of the Trieux extend up to 4 miles from the mainland, which in any case is low-lying hereabouts. Decca can give you confidence to press on if conditions close in, but don't forget the old adage about returning to the open sea rather than heading shorewards if uncertain of your position.

From the passage turning-point 3 miles W of Roches Douvres lighthouse, it is about 5 miles farther to Basse Crublent buoy and the entrance to the Tréguier River than it is to the outer approaches of the Trieux. However, when the tide is E-going and more or less contrary, those extra miles will be hard-gained.

St Helier to Granville

The passage from St Helier to Granville leads SE from Jersey for 30 miles, close N of Iles Chausey and down into the 'bottom right-hand corner' of the Gulf of St Malo. By leaving St Helier soon after local LW, you will carry the flood for most of the way, finally meeting a weak N-going stream between Chausey and the Normandy coast. In order to set off at LW, you have to come out of St Helier marina within 3 hours of HW and then wait at the holding pontoon in La Collette, just outside the main harbour.

Follow the Eastern Passage out of the Small Roads and take your departure from Demie de Pas

S-cardinal beacon tower, aiming to make good a track of 133°T. This will take you nearly 1 mile NE of the NE Minkies E-cardinal buoy, not quite 1½ miles NE of Les Ardentes E-cardinal buoy, a similar distance NE of L'État BW beacon, conspicuous on the NE edge of Chausey, and finally between two E-cardinal buoys a little way E of Chausey. From a position between these buoys, steer to round Pointe du Roc by ½ mile before turning E towards Granville Hérel marina.

In good visibility, other useful marks on the way down are: Gorey Castle on Jersey's E coast; L'Enseigne BW beacon, standing on a hump-backed islet about 1 mile N by W of Chausey's Grande Ile; Grande Ile lighthouse itself; and three rather similar E-cardinal beacon towers which guard the E perimeter of Chausey.

St Helier to Chausey, Cancale and St Malo

These are variations on the passage from St Helier to the NE Minkies buoy and then eastabout the Minkies but W of Chausey. There are several points to bear in mind, both on the first part of this route and later, depending on your destination.

1 It is vital to identify the NE Minkies buoy, coming right up with it before turning S between Chausey and the Minkies. Rounding the *N* Minkies buoy by mistake would have disastrous consequences.

2 On the leg between the Minkies and Chausey, aim to pass at least 2 miles W of Les Ardentes E-cardinal buoy, bearing in mind that drying patches straggle for nearly 1 mile W of the buoy.

3 If bound for St Malo, leave St Helier about 3 hours before local HW if you can average 5 knots. You will carry a fair tide down to the NE

Minkies buoy, push a weak foul stream between the Minkies and Chausey, and then pick up the first of the W-going ebb for the last stretch to St Malo.

4 If bound for Chausey Sound, either westabout Grande Ile or via the more intricate N entrance, leave St Helier not later than 2 hours after local LW, aiming to arrive near HW Chausey when the stream in the Sound is relatively slack.

5 If bound for Cancale, leave St Helier at LW, aiming to arrive off Pointe du Grouin soon after HW, while the stream is slack and there is plenty of depth in the approaches to Cancale.

St Helier to St Malo Westabout the Minkies

Although a couple of miles longer than skirting eastabout the Minkies, this route is more suitable during periods of springs when the tide will be ebbing as you leave St Helier in the morning and then making in the afternoon and evening. You will thus carry a fair stream through the Western Passage to Passage Rock N-cardinal buoy and have a broadly

favourable set down to the NW Minkies buoy. The tide should still be setting away from danger as you pass between the NW and SW Minkies, but the new flood will provide some help as you head SSE towards St Malo.

Spring streams are strong off St Malo; it is better to over- rather than under-compensate as you approach the coast, because you can always pass W of the two Vieux Banc buoys and enter St Malo via the Chenal de la Grande Porte. Le Grand Jardin RDF beacon is useful in poor visibility (*294.2kHz, 'GJ', 10M, Nos. 2, 6*).

St Helier to Lézardrieux

For this passage, I normally take a departure from Passage Rock buoy and then set a course to make good about 243°T for 32 miles, towards a position ½ mile due N of Basse du Nord N-cardinal buoy. This track leads 4 miles S of Barnouic E-cardinal beacon tower. If you leave St Helier ½ hour before local HW, the tide will be fairish throughout the trip if you average 5 knots, but you should aim to reach Basse du Nord before the flood starts setting E.

High-speed Factors

Passage legs between the Channel Islands and Brittany are short in motorboating terms. However, the rocks are numerous, the tides are strong and the area is susceptible to hazy visibility during the summer. You therefore need to plan your trips with care, making full use of Decca waypoints if you are so equipped.

St Peter Port to St Helier
This is about 1½ hours run at 20 knots. The ideal time to leave St Peter Port pierheads is 4 hours before HW, when the tide should be more or less astern all the way to St Helier. If you are coming straight out of Victoria Marina though, you won't be able to get away until 2½ hours or so before HW; in this case, you have to allow for some E-going stream between St Peter Port and the W coast of Jersey. Be sure to keep at least 1 mile off Corbière until you can line up for the

Western Passage into St Helier. There is a useful Racon beacon on the Western Passage leading line, but don't confuse it with the Demie de Pas Racon. Jersey, Sark and the S coast of Guernsey all show up well on radar.

St Peter Port to St Malo
This 55-mile passage is straightforward in quiet weather and reasonable visibility. The first leg is the 34 miles to the SW Minkies buoy, allowing carefully for tide and leaving the NW Minkies buoy ½

mile to the E. From the SW Minkies, turn SSE towards an offshore waypoint just N of the St Malo fairway buoy.

Cap Fréhel should appear as a bold radar target to starboard on this last leg, and Ile Cézembre usually shows up well fine on the port bow as you get down towards St Malo entrance.

St Peter Port to Lézardrieux or Tréguier

The 46-mile passage from St Peter Port to Lézardrieux should take 2½–3 hours in quiet conditions if you can average 15–20 knots. It is usually preferable to go westabout Roches Douvres, and a good time to leave St Peter Port is about 5 hours after local HW, when you will carry the last of the ebb SW from Guernsey, have fairly slack water as you pass Roches Douvres, and then pick up the first of the flood into the Lézardrieux River. If you are bound for Tréguier, leave 1 hour or so earlier in order to carry a W-going tide down off Les Heaux.

I always use two clearing waypoints when rounding Roches Douvres under power at speed—say, 4 miles NW of and 4 miles due W of the lighthouse. If you are bound for Lézardrieux, reach these waypoints in order and then set a course from the second to a landfall position 1 mile NW of Basse du Nord N-cardinal buoy. Keep track of your position as you approach the Lézardrieux River, because the powerful cross-tides between Les Heaux and La Horaine can confound even a fast motor-boat. If you are bound for the Tréguier River, you can work out a direct leg from the first Roches Douvres waypoint to a landfall position 1 mile due N of Basse Crublent red buoy.

The outer approaches to the Lézardrieux River can be rough with overfalls when the wind is against the tide, whereas conditions are often easier to the W of Les Heaux. Tréguier can also be a less stressful entrance than Lézardrieux in poor visibility, again because the cross-tides are not so strong. Whichever destination you choose, radar must be interpreted with great care, because the whole of this corner of North Brittany is low-lying, with dangers extending several miles seaward of the mainland coastline. Even Les Heaux lighthouse, which is tall but slim, is not a particularly reliable target.

St Helier to Granville

This 30-mile passage should take 1½–2 hours at 15–20 knots and it's best to leave St Helier soon after the marina gate opens, say 3 hours before HW. Aim to take your departure from ½ mile S of Demie de Pas beacon tower and work out a course to steer that will make good a track of 133°T. You will be partly dependent on traditional navigation for this passage, because Decca is subject to local errors in the area between Jersey and Granville. The following waypoints are useful to set, but be prepared for some slightly odd responses from your normally reliable display: (a) 1 mile NE of the NE Minkies E-cardinal buoy; (b) 1½ miles NE of Les Ardentes E-cardinal buoy; (c) 1½ miles NE of L'État BW beacon; (d) midway between the two E-cardinal buoys which lie a little way east of Chausey; (e) ½ mile SW of Pointe du Roc.

Iles Chausey provide a rather unreliable radar target until you get quite close, being very low-lying. As you draw E of Chausey, the Normandy coast and Pointe du Roc show up well.

St Helier to St Malo, Chausey or Cancale

If you are bound for St Malo eastabout the Minkies and can average 15–20 knots, leave St Helier 2–2½ hours before HW. The first leg is from Demie de Pas beacon tower to the NE Minkies buoy, the second leg to a position ¾ mile E of the SE Minkies buoy, and the final leg down to the St Malo fairway buoy. Ile Cézembre is a good radar target on the approach to St Malo.

If you are bound for Chausey Sound via the Entrée de la Déroute, leave St Helier an hour before HW and make for the NE Minkies buoy first. On the second leg SSW from the NE Minkies buoy, be sure to pass at least 2 miles W of Les Ardentes E-cardinal buoy, to avoid the drying patches which extend for nearly 1 mile W of the buoy. Watch out for crab-pot markers in this area.

St Helier to Cancale is about 34 miles via the NE Minkies buoy and the Entrée de la Déroute. Leave St Helier about 2 hours before HW, aiming to arrive off Pointe du Grouin near HW when the stream is slack and there is plenty of water in the approaches to Cancale. Pointe du Grouin provides a good radar target from northward, but merges with Ile des Landes until you get close.

St Helier to St Malo westabout the Minkies

Fast motor-boats bound from St Helier to St Malo tend to be better off skirting eastabout the Minkies via the Entrée de la Déroute. It is a couple of miles shorter this way, but the main advantage is that the sea is often quieter, with the Minkies forming a natural breakwater to any westerly swell. However, the westabout route is more straightforward in poor visibility, when you can follow the Western Passage out to Passage Rock N-cardinal buoy and then make three legs in fairly open water to the NW Minkies, the SW Minkies and St Malo fairway buoys.

As far as tidal streams are concerned, a good time to set off on this passage is about 5½ hours after HW St Helier, which gives you a weak fair stream out to Passage Rock buoy but then only a slight cross-set as you come round the Minkies. Even if you make 20 knots in open water, you can probably reckon on 2½–3 hours 'from door to door' by the time you have negotiated the pilotage at either end. You would therefore be arriving in St Malo with plenty of water over the sill at St Servan marina, or just in time for the first lock into the Bassin Vauban.

Cap Fréhel should appear as a bold radar target to starboard on the last leg from the SW Minkies, and Ile Cezembre usually shows up well fine on the port bow as you get down towards St Malo entrance.

St Helier to Lézardrieux

The total distance from St Helier to Lézardrieux is 48 miles, but the open sea part of the trip from Passage Rock N-cardinal buoy to Basse du Nord N-cardinal buoy is only 32 miles, which is about 1½–2 hours at 15–20 knots. If it can be arranged, you are best arriving off the Trieux estuary near slack water, so that you don't have to cope with the powerful cross-tides that run in the offing between Les Heaux and La Horaine. These streams can make it difficult for a stranger to pilot his way safely into the estuary and can also cause nasty patches of overfalls in even quite moderate winds.

With these factors in mind, a good time to cast off from St Helier Marina is near the sill closing time, 3 hours after local HW (don't leave it any later though, or you will be locked in for another tide). The stream will be fair out to Passage Rock buoy and all the way across to Lézardrieux. Set your landfall waypoint for ½ mile due N of Basse du Nord buoy. This track leads about 4 miles S of Barnouic E-cardinal beacon tower, but Barnouic is rather short and doesn't always come up well on radar.

The landfall coastline is very low-lying and usually difficult to interpret on a radar screen until you get right in among all the dangers, although La Horaine lighthouse shows up well from some distance offshore.

Pilot Books, etc.

Admiralty NP27, *The Channel Pilot*.

Admiralty NP74, *List of Lights, Vol. A*.

Channel Harbours and Anchorages, K. Adlard Coles, 6th edn 1985, published by Nautical.

North Brittany Pilot, K. Adlard Coles and the RCC Pilotage Foundation, 5th edn (rev.) 1984, published by Adlard Coles.

Channel Island Pilot, M. Robson, 4th edn 1990, published by Nautical.

French Pilot, Omonville to Tréguier, M. Robson, 1983 edn, published by Nautical.

The Shell Pilot to the English Channel, J. Coote, vol. 2, 1987 edn, published by Faber and Faber.

The Cruising Association Handbook, 7th edn 1990, published by the Cruising Association.

Channel Islands and North Brittany Cruising, P. Cumberlidge, 1st edn 1990, published by Yachting Monthly.

Normandy and Channel Island Pilot, M. Brackenbury, 7th edn (revised) 1990, published by Adlard Coles.

Adlard Coles Pilot Pack, Vol. 3, B. Goulder, 1st edn 1989, published by Adlard Coles.

Charts

Admiralty:

No. 2669—The Channel Islands and adjacent coast of France

No. 808—East Guernsey, Herm and Sark

No. 3670—Les Sept Iles to L'Ost Pic

No. 3655—Jersey and adjacent coast of France

No. 1137—Approaches to St Helier

No. 3656—Plateau des Minquiers and adjacent coast of France

No. 3659—Cap Fréhel to Iles Chausey

No. 3672—Harbours on the NW coast of France

No. 3673—Lézardrieux and Paimpol with approaches

No. 3674—L'Ost Pic to Cap Fréhel

No. 2700—Port St Malo and approaches

Imray:

C33A—Channel Islands, North

C33B—Channel Islands, South

Stanford:

No. 16—The Channel Islands

Tidal Atlases

Admiralty NP264, *The Channel Islands and adjacent coast of France*.

Stanford's Tidal Atlas, English Channel West.

Tidal Streams (times based on HW Dover)

Position	E-going stream starts	W-going stream starts
3 miles W of Roches Douvres lighthouse	+0230	−0215
Trieux estuary, near the Basse du Nord buoy	+0135	−0440
Jersey, close S of Noirmont Point	+0215	−0430
Near the NE Minkies buoy	+0220	−0400
Near the St Malo fairway buoy	+0145	−0430

	N-going stream starts	S-going stream starts
Little Russel, just outside St Peter Port	+0450	−0130
Jersey, 2 miles W of Grosnez Point	−0450	+0120
Between Chausey and Granville	+0600	−0020

Tidal Differences and Heights

Place	Time of HW on Dover	Heights above chart datum in metres			
		MHWS	MLWS	MHWN	MLWN
St Peter Port	−0440	9.0	1.0	6.7	3.5
St Helier	−0450	11.1	1.3	8.1	4.1
Chausey Sound	−0505	12.6	1.5	9.7	4.4
Granville	−0505	12.8	1.4	9.6	4.6
Cancale	−0505	13.3	2.0	10.1	5.1
St Malo	−0510	12.1	1.4	9.1	4.4
Les Heaux	−0520	9.8	1.0	7.5	3.4
Lézardrieux	−0415	10.0	0.9	7.5	3.4

Important Lights

Guernsey:

Bréhon fort (*Iso, 4s, 9M*); Castle Breakwater head (*Alt. WR, 10s, 16M, vis 187°-007°T*); White Rock pierhead (*OcG, 5s, 14M, intens 174°-354°T*); St Martin's Point, SE tip of Guernsey (*Fl3, WR, 10s, 14M; R vis 185°-191°T, W vis 191°-011°T, R vis 011°-081°T*); Les Hanois, lighthouse off the SW tip of Guernsey (*Q2, 5s, 23M, vis 294°-237°T*).

Jersey:

Grosnez Point (*Fl2, WR, 15s, 19M, 17M; W vis 081°-188°T, R vis 188°-241°T, obscured elsewhere*); La Corbière (*Iso, WR, 10s, 17M, 16M; W vis shore-294°T, R vis 294°-328°T, W vis 328°-148°T, R vis 148°T-shore*); Noirmont Point (*Fl4, 12s, 13M*); Western Passage leading lights in line 082°T—*front* La Grève d'Azette (*Oc5s, 14M, vis 034°-129°T*), *rear* Mont Ubé (*Alt. WR, 6s, 12M, vis 250°-095°T*); Platte lattice beacon (*FlR, 1½s, 5M*); St Helier (Small Roads) leading lights in line 023°T, synchronized—*front* Albert Pier elbow (*OcG, 5s, 11M*), *rear* Esplanade (*OcR, 5s, 12M*); Demie de Pas (*Mo 'D' WR, 12s, 14M, 10M; R vis 130°-303°T, W vis 303°-130°T*); Gorey pierhead (*OcRG, 5s, 12M; R vis 304°-352°T, G vis 352°-304°T*).

Chausey, Granville and Cancale:

Grande Ile lighthouse (*Fl, 5s, 25M*); La Crabière-Est (*OcWRG, 4s, 7M, 5M, 3M; W vis 079°-291°T, G vis 291°-329°T, W vis 329°-335°T, R vis 335°-079°T*); Le Pignon E-cardinal beacon tower (*Oc2, WR, 6s, 11M, 8M; R vis 005°-150°T, W vis 150°-005°T*); Pointe du Roc lighthouse (*Fl4, 15s, 23M*); Hérel Marina Digue Principale (*FlR, 4s, 7M*); Pierre de Herpin lighthouse (*Oc2, 6s, 15M*); Cancale pierhead (*Oc3, G, 12s, 7M*).

St Malo to Les Heaux:

Le Grand Jardin (*Fl2R, 10s, 15M*)—in line with La Balue (*FG, 25M*) bearing 130°T, leads through the Chenal de la Petite Porte, and in line with Rochebonne (*FR, 25M*) bearing 089°T, leads through the Chenal de la Grande Porte; Cap Fréhel (*Fl2, 10s, 29M*); Grand Léjon (*Fl5, WR, 20s, 15M, 12M; R vis 015°-058°T, W vis 058°-283°T,*

R vis 283°-250°T, W vis 350°-015°T*); L'Ost Pic (*OcWR, 4s, 10M, 7M, W vis 105°-116°T, R vis 116°-221°T, W vis 221°-253°T, R vis 253°-291°T, W vis 291°-329°T*); Rosédo (*Fl, 5s, 23M*); Pointe du Paon (*FWRG, 11M, 8M, 7M; W vis 033°-078°T, G vis 078°-181°T, W vis 181°-196°T, R vis 196°-307°T, W vis 307°-316°T, R vis 316°-348°T*); La Horaine (*Fl3, 12s, 10M*); Plateau de Barnouic E-cardinal beacon tower (*VQ3, 5s, 9M*); Roches Douvres (*Fl, 5s, 29M*); Les Heaux de Bréhat (*Oc3, WRG, 12s, 15M, 12M, 10M; R vis 227°-247°T, W vis 247°-270°T, G vis 270°-302°T, W vis 302°-227°T*).

RDF Beacons

Guernsey aero beacon (*361kHz, 'GUR', 30M, cont.*); St Peter Port, Castle breakwater (*285kHz, 'GY', 10M, cont.*); Jersey West aero beacon (*329kHz, 'JW', 25M, cont.*); La Corbière (*305.7kHz, 'CB', 20M, Nos. 2, 4, 6*); St Helier approaches, Elizabeth Castle (*287.3kHz, 'EC', 10M, cont.*); Jersey East aero beacon (*367kHz, 'JEY', 75M, cont.*); Granville aero beacon (*321kHz, 'GV', 25M, cont.*); Le Grand Jardin lighthouse (*294.2kHz, 'GJ', 10M, Nos. 2, 6*); Cap Fréhel (*305.7kHz, 'FÉ', 20M, Nos. 1, 3, 5*); Rosédo, Ile de Bréhat (*294.2kHz, 'DO', 10M, Nos. 1, 5*); Roches Douvres (*298.8kHz, 'RD', 70M, No. 4*).

Weather Forecasts (all times GMT except where otherwise stated)

BBC shipping forecast area:

Portland

VHF coast radio stations:

Jersey Radio—0645, 0745, 1245, 1845, 2245, on Chs 25 and 82

St Malo—0633, 1133, on Ch. 2

Paimpol—0633, 1133, on Ch. 84

Recorded telephone forecast:

Tel. 0481 64033

Met Office forecasts:

Jersey Airport Met Office, Tel. 0534 23660 or 46111

9 DARTMOUTH TO LES HEAUX DE BRÉHAT

The tall, slender lighthouse of Les Heaux stands at the end of a formidable plateau of drying rocks which stretches seawards from Brittany's N tip. For many yachtsmen coming from England, Les Heaux offers a first tangible glimpse of the 'Côte de Granit Rose', that wild, attractive and tide-swept littoral bounded on the E by Ile de Bréhat and on the W by Les Sept Iles.

The direct track from Dartmouth to Les Heaux is about 88 miles at 168°T, a longish cross-Channel passage which can be relaxing in a moderate north-westerly, fast and invigorating in a brisk westerly, and an undoubtedly hard slog in a fresh south-westerly. It leads you out between the friendly twin castles at the mouth of the Dart, S past the Skerries Bank and Start Point, and then through a wide band of busy shipping lanes. The last third of the passage takes you into a rather empty area of sea about 20 miles W of Guernsey, and finally 10–12 miles W of the inhospitable Plateau de Roches Douvres and the much smaller Plateau de Barnouic.

There is no denying that, in boisterous weather or poor visibility, the landfall can be somewhat daunting. Most of the navigational tension is due to the powerful Brittany tides and the fact that off-lying

dangers extend up to 3 miles from the mainland proper. It is important, therefore, to have a reliable estimate of your position before closing the coast.

However, the rewards of successfully completing this passage are considerable. Having arrived off Les Heaux, you have an immediate choice of two equally fascinating Brittany rivers, depending on the state of the tide. If the stream is E-going, it is usually wise to carry it round the few miles to the Trieux estuary, tucking upstream as far as the sleepy little town of Lézardrieux or edging into one of the anchorages off Ile de Bréhat. If the stream is W-going, you have the picturesque Tréguier River a similar distance down-tide.

The timing of this cross-Channel passage is not too critical, but is worth some consideration if, like me, you are keen to keep life as uncomplicated as possible. I have made the trip in a fair range of conditions and have left Dartmouth at various different times of day or night and yet, browsing through the logs just recently, I came across one copy-book crossing which was probably as nearly ideal as one is ever likely to achieve.

The early morning shipping forecast for sea areas Portland and Plymouth was giving NW 3 or 4, with the weather fair and visibility moderate becoming

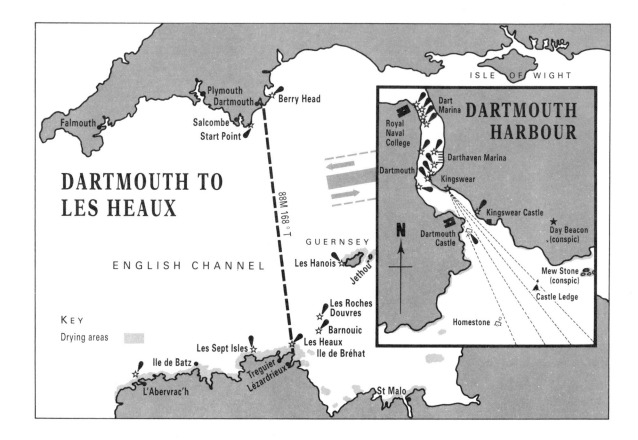

good later. Conditions looked generally settled for the next couple of days and the barometer had risen to 1022. We had a leisurely breakfast, picked up some fresh stores from town, topped up with water and slipped the moorings soon after 1100.

The light north-westerly carried us gently downstream and between the two familiar castles. The Homestone buoy was abreast at noon and the wind gradually gathered weight as we cleared the Devon coast. With the mainsail squared away on the port side, a preventer rigged and the jib just asleep, *Stormalong* was slipping easily through the water at 5 knots. This happy state of affairs continued unchanged for the next 20 hours.

Visibility was excellent and we made good pro-gress out into the Channel, clearing the main shipping lanes during the last of the daylight. At 2200 we picked up the loom of Les Hanois, about 25 miles away on the SW tip of Guernsey. The resulting position line tallied nicely with the EP, putting us a shade farther on.

The night was clear, and as warm as English Channel nights ever seem to be. By 0300, the powerful light on Roches Douvres was bearing due E, with Les Heaux occulting dead ahead and Les Sept Iles visible to the SW. A respectable cocked-hat put us pretty much where we ought to be and I snatched a last fix at 0420 before Roches Douvres and Sept Iles faded in the twilight. It was now 2 hours after local LW and a strong E-going stream

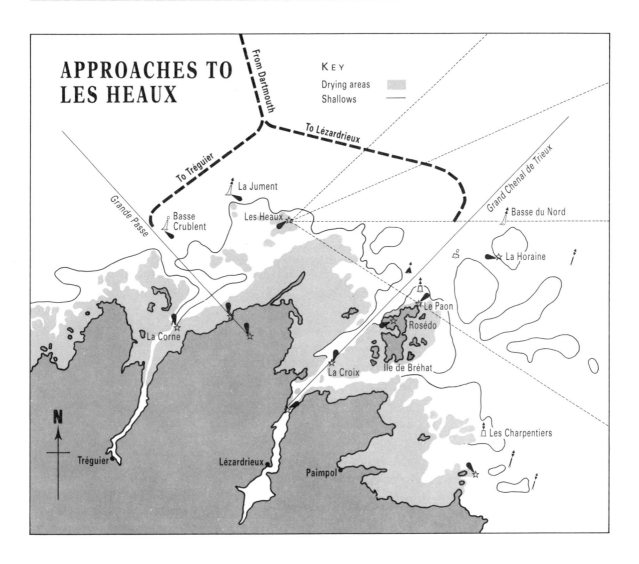

APPROACHES TO
LES HEAUX

KEY

Drying areas

Shallows

From Dartmouth

To Lézardrieux

To Tréguier

Grande Passe

Grand Chenal de Trieux

La Jument

Basse
Crublent

Les Heaux

Basse du Nord

La Horaine

Le Paon

Rosédo

La Corne

La Croix

Ile de Bréhat

N

Les Charpentiers

Tréguier

Lézardrieux

Paimpol

was running. We therefore bore away for La
Horaine tower and the Grand Chenal de Trieux.
By 0800 *Stormalong* was anchored just below
Lézardrieux, the coffee percolating and some excel-
lent home-cured bacon sizzling on the stove.

There are several advantages in making the passage from Dartmouth to Les Heaux according to a
similar schedule.

1 Leaving at a civilized hour of the day means that
you can have the benefit of a long, uninterrupted
night's rest. There is also plenty of time in the
morning for last-minute shopping, topping up
with water or fuel, and ringing the local met
office if you have any doubts about the weather.

2 There is a whole afternoon during which your
crew can settle into cruising routine before the
night part of the passage.

3 If you can keep up an average of 5 knots, you

should be clear of the mid-Channel shipping lanes by nightfall. You'll also be well placed to pick up Les Hanois light (*Q2, 5s*) as you pass Guernsey, which can provide a useful check on progress.

4 It will still be dark as you fetch Roches Douvres (*Fl, 5s*). When this powerful light is abeam, you should also be able to see Les Heaux (*Occ3, WRG, 12s*) and Les Sept Iles (*Fl3, 15s*). These three can give a series of fixes as you close the coast.

5 Dawn should be breaking as you finally approach Les Heaux, just in time for the pilotage into Lézardrieux or Tréguier.

If you make nearer 4 knots than 5, you will need to leave Dartmouth at about 0700 to be arriving off Les Heaux at the same sort of time. If you can average 6 knots, you can delay your departure until after lunch, slipping your berth at about 1400.

The tide sets across your track on this passage, and doesn't materially affect your departure time provided you are not too concerned about whether you end up at Tréguier or Lézardrieux. My strategy has always been to make for Les Heaux and then turn E or W depending on how the stream is running when I arrive. Given the choice though, the landfall in the vicinity of Les Heaux is generally more straightforward during a period of neaps. At springs, the streams can reach 5 or 6 knots in the outer approaches to Lézardrieux, keeping the navigator on edge and kicking up some rather nasty patches of overfalls.

At dead neaps, HW at Dartmouth is around the middle of the day. Working on an 1100 departure time, you will be picking up the first of the weak foul stream in Start Bay. This will be running for nearly 5 hours after you clear the harbour entrance, and you then have a full 6 hours of W-going stream and

a full 6 hours of E-going. As you arrive off Les Heaux, the W-going stream will just be starting again and Tréguier will probably be a more practical destination than Lézardrieux. Pass N of La Jument buoy and make for Basse Crublent buoy at the entrance to the Tréguier River. If you are set on Lézardrieux, make your landfall a good 5 miles E of Les Heaux, so that (a) you are well in position for the Grand Chenal, and (b) you have enough room to counteract the W-going stream as you come in.

If you make the passage during a period of spring tides and keep broadly to the same timing, the stream will be E-going as you arrive off Les Heaux. It will therefore be hard work to reach Tréguier, but you can easily slip down towards La Horaine so as to line up for the Grand Chenal de Trieux and then carry the flood up to Lézardrieux or Bréhat.

Bad weather *en route*

It can sometimes happen that you set off from Dartmouth towards Les Heaux with a fair westerly, and then find yourself headed part-way across when a warm front swings up the Channel to back and freshen the wind. If you get caught like this and don't want to be slogging to windward, St Peter Port offers a snug bolt-hole. Under such conditions, it is usually best to shape a course for Les Hanois and come southabout Guernsey round St Martin's Point.

Deteriorating visibility is the real curse when approaching the North Brittany coast, although the magical Decca can now take some of the worry out of a murky landfall. For those low-tech navigators like myself, the powerful RDF beacon on Roches Douvres (*298.8kHz, 'RD', 70M, No. 4*) can help confirm your distance off as you approach Les Heaux. I have also used its back-bearing to home into the Grand Chenal de Trieux until the low-powered RDF beacon at Rosédo, on the NW side of Ile de Bréhat, has come within accurate range (*294.2kHz, 'DO', 10M, Nos. 1 and 5*).

If the weather is really thick, it is obviously more prudent to stand off into safe water than to grope your way among the numerous rocks fringing the Côte de Granit Rose. If the visibility is patchy though, there is something to be said for making your landfall to the W of the entrance to the Tréguier River. The tidal streams are not quite so vicious as those off the Trieux estuary and the 5-mile stretch of coast between, say, Pointe du Château and the Basse Guazer whistle buoy can just about be closed to within 1½ miles. This gives you a better margin of visibility than the area around Les Heaux, where the safe limit of a blind approach is more like 3 miles.

The Return Passage

Ideally, the return crossing to Dartmouth should be made with some S in the wind. As far as tides are concerned, it is usually best to leave Tréguier or Lézardrieux soon after local HW. This gives you a fair run down-river and, by the time you reach the entrance, the Channel ebb will be just under way. In the next 4 or 5 hours, you should therefore be set 10 miles or so to the W, with two possible benefits: (a) in westerly weather, a good shove to windward on this side of the Channel will improve your slant for the rest of the passage, and (b) you will be carried well clear of Barnouic and Roches Douvres, whereas an equivalent easterly set from a powerful flood tide would put you perilously close to these dangers.

Keep St Peter Port in mind in case the weather deteriorates from the W during the early part of the passage, although an initial tidal set down-Channel will put Guernsey some distance away. Planning your landfall for Dartmouth entrance tends to be a better strategy than heading for Start Point first. With the latter, you risk missing the tide and picking up a foul stream for the last 12 miles. By making directly for Dartmouth, you avoid the stronger streams and the race off Start, and you also keep a lighthouse and RDF beacon on either hand—Start Point to port (*Fl3, 10s, 25M: RDF 298.8kHz, 'SP', 70M, No. 2*) and Berry Head to starboard (*Fl2, 15s, 18M: RDF 318kHz, 'BHD', 25M, cont.*). Bearings of these two give a reasonable cut for position fixing as you approach the coast. In daylight, the mouth of the Dart can easily be located by the conspicuous 'day-mark' on its E side.

In easterly weather, Salcombe is an alternative if you can't lay the course for Dartmouth, especially if you arrive off Start Point feeling rather battered with wind and tide against you. In poor visibility it is fairly safe to approach the coast anywhere between Dartmouth and Salcombe but, if conditions are very murky, don't attempt either entrance unless you have Decca to help you. The best plan in dense fog is to arrive in Start Bay with the aid of RDF and then to sound in towards its S shore, anchoring anywhere between Beesands and the N end of Slapton Sands. Start Point's fog-horn will be useful as you feel your way in.

High-speed Factors

If you can average 15 knots, the passage from Dartmouth entrance to an offshore waypoint 5 miles due N of Les Heaux lighthouse should take just over 5½ hours. You need to watch out for crab-pot buoys off the Devon coast, especially to the E and S of Start Point. You can expect to meet the first of the up-Channel shipping after about 1 hour and the total width of the traffic lanes will be something like 30 miles.

It is worth setting an intermediate waypoint somewhere not far S of where you emerge from the lanes, perhaps a position with Les Hanois lighthouse, off the SW tip of Guernsey, bearing 100°T distant 20–25 miles. With a Guernsey W waypoint 2 miles due S of Les Hanois lighthouse and a Guernsey E waypoint 1¼ miles S of St Martin's lighthouse, you are then prepared to break off for St Peter Port, southabout Guernsey, if the weather should freshen from the W on passage, or it looks as though there might be poor visibility on the North Brittany coast. The S coast of Guernsey shows up clearly on radar from the W.

As you approach the Brittany offshore waypoint, you can decide whether to alter to the SW, for La Crublent red buoy at the entrance to the Tréguier River, or to the SE, for a position 1 mile NW of Basse du Nord N-cardinal buoy, at the outer end of the Grand Chenal de Trieux. Much will depend upon sea state, visibility, and whether the tide is setting W or E.

The outer approaches to the Lézardrieux River can be rough with overfalls during the middle hours of a weather-going spring tide, whereas conditions are often easier to the W of Les Heaux. Tréguier can also be an easier entrance than Lézardrieux in poor visibility, again because the cross-tides are not quite so powerful as they are between Les Heaux and La Horaine. Whichever destination you choose, radar must be interpreted with great care, because the whole of this corner of North Brittany is low-lying, with dangers extending several miles seaward of the mainland coastline. Even Les Heaux lighthouse, which is tall but slim, is not a particularly reliable target.

Pilot Books, etc.

Admiralty NP27, *The Channel Pilot.*

Admiralty NP74, *List of Lights, Vol. A.*

North Brittany Pilot, K. Adlard Coles and the RCC Pilotage foundation, 5th edn (rev.) 1984, published by Adlard Coles.

French Pilot, vol. 1, M. Robson, 1983 edn, published by Nautical.

The Shell Pilot to the English Channel, J. Coote, vols 1 and 2, 1987 edns, published by Faber and Faber.

Adlard Coles Pilot Pack, Vol. 3, B. Goulder, 1st edn 1989, published by Adlard Coles.

Channel Islands and North Brittany Cruising, P. Cumberlidge, 1st edn 1990, published by Yachting Monthly.

The Cruising Association Handbook, 7th edn 1990, published by the Cruising Association.

Charts

Admiralty:

No. 2675—English Channel

No. 1634—Salcombe to Brixham

No. 3670—Les Sept Iles to L'Ost-Pic

No. 3672—Harbours on the NW Coast of France (which includes the Tréguier River from La Corne lighthouse to the Marina)

No. 3673—Lézardrieux and Paimpol with approaches

Imray:

C10—Western English Channel Passage Chart

Y43—Exmouth to Salcombe

C34—Cap d'Erquy to Ile de Batz (rather small-scale for making a landfall on Les Heaux)

Stanford:

No. 2—English Channel, Western Section (suitable for the main part of the passage)

Tidal Atlases

Stanford's Tidal Atlas, English Channel West (recommended)

Admiralty NP250, *English and Bristol Channels.*

Admiralty NP264, *The Channel Islands and Adjacent Coasts of France.*

Tidal Streams (times based on HW Dover)

Position	E-going stream starts	W-going stream starts
Off Dartmouth	+0540	−0100
Off Start Point	+0500	−0115
3 miles N of Les Heaux	+0230	−0345

Tidal Differences and Heights

Place	Time of HW on Dover	MHWS	MLWS	MHWN	MLWN
			Heights above chart datum in metres		
Dartmouth	−0515	4.8	0.4	3.6	1.8
Les Heaux	−0520	9.8	1.0	7.5	3.4
Lézardrieux	−0415	10.0	0.9	7.5	3.4
Tréguier	−0545	9.7	0.9	7.4	3.3

Important Lights

Devon coast:

Berry Head (*Fl2, 15s, 18M*); Dart entrance sector light at Kingswear (*IsoWRG, 3s, 8M*); Start Point (*Fl3, 10s, 25M*); Salcombe entrance sector light at Sandhill Point (*DirFl, WRG, 2s, 10M, 7M, 7M*).

On passage:

Channel Light Vessel (*Fl, 15s, 25M*); Les Hanois (*Q2, 5s, 23M*); Roches Douvres (*Fl, 5s, 29M*); Barnouic Tower (*VQ3, 5s, 9M*).

Brittany coast:

Les Heaux (*Oc3, WRG, 12s, 15M, 12M, 10M*); La Horaine (*Fl3, 12s, 10M*); Les Sept Iles (*Fl3, 15s, 24M*); Grand Chenal de Trieux leading lights in line 225°T—*front* at La Croix (*Oc4s, 19M*), *rear* at Bodic (*QFl, intens 222°-229°T*); Grande Passe de Tréguier leading lights in line—*front* at Port de la Chaine (*Oc4s, 12M*), *rear* at Sainte-Antoine (*OcR, 4s, 15M*).

RDF Beacons

Devon coast:

Berry Head (*318kHz, 'BHD', 25M, cont.*); Start Point (*298.8kHz, 'SP', 70M, No. 2*).

On passage:

Channel Light Vessel (*287.3kHz, 'CR', 10M, cont.*); Casquets lighthouse (*298.8kHz, 'QS', 50M, No. 3*); Guernsey aero beacon (*361kHz, 'GUR', 30M, cont.*); Roches Douvres (*298.8kHz, 'RD', 70M, No. 4*

Brittany coast:

Rosédo lighthouse on Ile de Bréhat (*294.2kHz, 'DO', 10M, Nos. 1 and 5*).

Weather Forecasts (all times GMT except where otherwise stated)

BBC shipping forecast areas:

Portland, Plymouth

VHF coast radio stations:

Start Point—0803, 2003, on Ch. 26
Jersey Radio—0645, 0745, 1245, 1845, 2245, on Chs 25 and 82
Paimpol—0633, 1133, on Ch. 84

Marinecall:

Tel. 0898 500 458

Local radio coastal forecasts:

BBC Radio Devon—shipping forecasts Mon–Fri at local times 0605, 0833, 1310, 1733; Sat at 0605, 0633, 0833, 1310; Sun at 0833, 1310. Frequencies: Torbay—*1458 kHz, 206m, 103.4 MHz FM*; Plymouth—*855 kHz, 351m, 103.4 MHz FM*; ILR Torbay (Devonair Radio)—coastguard forecast every day at 0830 local time; small craft warnings when given, on the hour, every hour. Frequencies: *954 kHz, 314m, 97.0 MHz FM*

Met Office forecasts:

Plymouth Weather Centre, Tel. 0752 402534

10 PLYMOUTH TO L'ABERVRAC'H

When I was mulling over some of the important points to bear in mind when planning this particular cross-Channel passage, it struck me that many of them are more or less valid whether you take your departure from Plymouth or from one of the other West Country havens such as Dartmouth, Salcombe, Newton Ferrers, Fowey, Falmouth or the Helford River.

Of course distances vary a little. Dartmouth entrance to Le Libenter buoy off L'Abervrac'h is the longest crossing—about 111 miles, whereas if you leave from Falmouth or Helford, it is a more modest 87 miles from a position 1 mile E of the Manacles buoy to Le Libenter. You'll also get a different slant; Falmouth to L'Abervrac'h is an easy reach in a due westerly, but the passage from Dartmouth is a closer-hauled proposition.

For the return trip, none of the main South Devon or Cornish harbours is difficult to get into, but Plymouth is probably the most straightforward of them all, with its wide well-marked entrance, its deep-water roadstead, and the Eddystone light as a useful outlying sentinel. It is equally easy of access in heavy onshore weather, something to bear in mind if you are dodging depressions on the way home from Brittany. In fog, too, there is no real

problem about approaching Plymouth Sound, and if you finally home in on the Penlee Point radiobeacon, the soundings give you a clear indication when you are within ¼ mile of land.

But first to L'Abervrac'h, that attractive rocky estuary at the extreme W end of Brittany's rugged N coast. Here you will find a traditional staging post for English yachts bound S through the Chenal du Four or on their way home after a Biscay cruise. For L'Abervrac'h is, undoubtedly, a handy port-of-call. It offers good shelter from all quarters once you are safely inside, and is accessible by day or night, at any state of tide, and in most weathers. Just off the entrance is the tall and prominent lighthouse on Ile Vierge, which also has a powerful radiobeacon (*298.8kHz, 'VG', 70M, No. 5*).

The crossing from Plymouth to L'Abervrac'h is not all that difficult navigationally, but it does have some potentially daunting characteristics. For example, the fact that you are striking out for the very tip of Brittany can make the passage feel somewhat lonely. As you draw well away from the friendly green shores of Devon and Cornwall, it is not unusual to experience a heightened awareness of the scale and power of the sea. Out to the W there is nothing but empty ocean for thousands of miles;

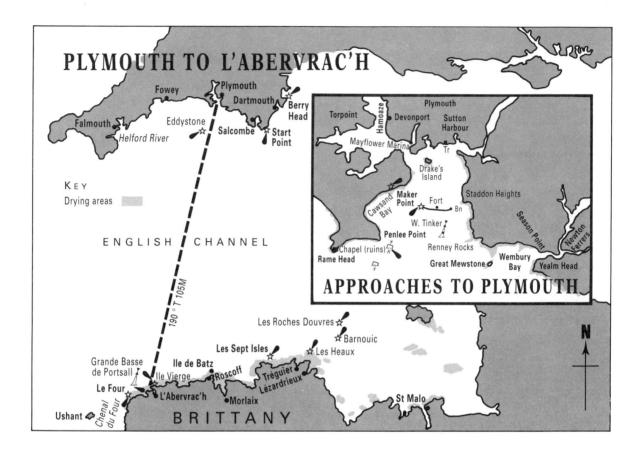

PLYMOUTH TO L'ABERVRAC'H

Fowey • Plymouth • Dartmouth • Berry Head

Falmouth • Eddystone • Salcombe • Start Point

Helford River

K E Y

Drying areas

E N G L I S H   C H A N N E L

190° T 105M

APPROACHES TO PLYMOUTH

Torpoint • Hamoaze • Devonport • Plymouth • Sutton Harbour

Mayflower Marina • Tr

Drake's Island

Cawsand Bay • Maker Point • Fort • Bn • Staddon Heights

W. Tinker

Penlee Point • Season Point • Newton Ferrers

Chapel (ruins) • Renney Rocks

Rame Head • Great Mewstone • Wembury Bay • Yealm Head

Les Roches Douvres

Barnouic

Les Sept Isles • Les Heaux

Grande Basse de Portsall • Ile de Batz • Roscoff

Le Four • Ile Vierge • Tréguier Lézardrieux

L'Abervrac'h • Morlaix • St Malo

Ushant • Chenal du Four

B R I T T A N Y

N

across the Channel is the North Brittany coast, which can be a tricky enough landfall anywhere along its length in bad weather; and somewhere right ahead is the local 'end of the earth', flanked by the rather bleak, tide-swept waters around Ushant.

The passage leads across a broad shipping route between the Ushant and Casquets separation zones. You are vulnerable to traffic for something like 45 miles from about mid-Channel onwards and this distance increases to nearer 60 miles if you leave from Dartmouth. The crossing from Falmouth involves the cleanest cut across these lanes. As you begin to approach the NW corner of Finistère, a long and slightly menacing Atlantic swell will probably make its presence felt, underlining your

exposed position and warning you not to dawdle.

Poor visibility is not uncommon around this part of the Brittany coast, particularly in high summer when a haze is apt to settle over the land just before dawn and not burn off until well into the morning. For this reason, there is often much to be said for aiming to make your landfall in the early afternoon, when the chances of reasonable visibility are fairly high but there is still plenty of daylight left for the final approach and the pilotage into L'Abervrac'h.

This timing also fits in well with the rest of the passage. Suppose, for example, you plan to be 6 miles off the Brittany coast by 1400. Working back at an average speed of 5 knots would put you just entering the N edge of the shipping lanes at around

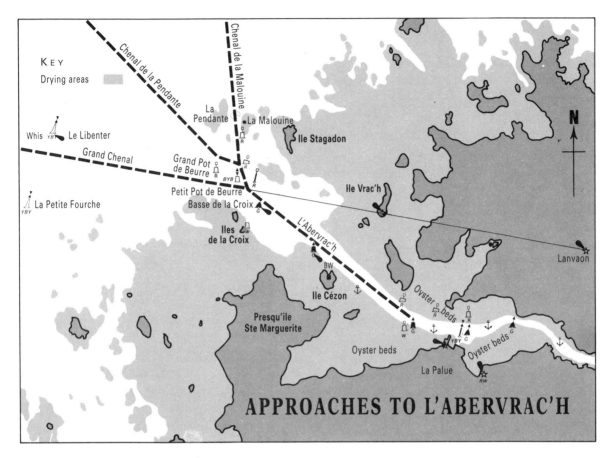

APPROACHES TO L'ABERVRAC'H

dawn, giving you full daylight for the main period of tanker dodging.

To keep this schedule, you would have to be passing Plymouth breakwater not later than 1800, not a bad departure time if you can imagine the scene. You'd be slipping your berth from Sutton Harbour or Mayflower Marina at 1700, say, having had a good snooze after lunch and had ample time to prepare for sea. You might have put together a tasty casserole earlier in the day, of which you could partake while still in the relative shelter of Plymouth Sound. You'd pick up the shipping forecast at 1750 and the general weather forecast at 1755, which together would give you a good picture of what to expect in the next 24 hours.

It should still be daylight as you pass a couple of miles to the E of the Eddystone, but its two friendly flashes would provide a useful back-bearing as you started to draw well offshore. Given good visibility, you'd be able to see the Lizard light away to the W and Start Point to the NE.

You'd probably cross some inshore shipping at dusk, bound between the Lizard and Start, but the hours of darkness ought to be fairly clear of traffic, except for the occasional fishing boat. Come the dawn, you could expect to pick up the first of the up-Channel shipping in the main lanes and be kept on your toes until about midday. An early lunch perhaps, in readiness for the landfall, and then, if you were lucky, the tall lighthouse on Ile Vierge would emerge from the haze a shade to the E of S.

If land is elusive, Ile Vierge RDF beacon (*298.8kHz, 'VG', 70M, No. 5*) is useful, especially when crossed with Ushant's Créac'h beacon (*308.0kHz, 'CA', 100M, No. 6*). These two give the best cut if you are closing the coast W of L'Abervrac'h, when you are about 10 miles due N of Basse de Portsall N-cardinal buoy. I often aim to make my landfall in the vicinity of this buoy because, depending on what the tide is doing as you arrive, you have the option of either turning E for the last few miles to Le Libenter or else carrying on through the Chenal du Four.

Poor Visibility

If it is murky as you make your landfall, do not despair. Shape your course towards Basse de Portsall buoy and the decreasing bearing of Ile Vierge beacon will give you a fair idea of your progress. If you can pick up Basse de Portsall's mournful whistle and sail right up to the buoy, you are half-way home and dry. The tide will then determine whether you should turn left for L'Abervrac'h or carry on S for Le Four.

Either course of action is feasible provided you start from right alongside Basse de Portsall buoy and keep a careful DR. It is not too difficult to pick your way down through the Chenal du Four in quite thick weather. Le Four lighthouse can be passed close on its W side, so long as you approach it from W of N. It has a very distinctive fog siren (*3+2, 75s*).

In poor visibility, getting into L'Abervrac'h from Basse de Portsall requires some careful plotting and a determination to return to sea if you cannot find Le Libenter buoy. This W-cardinal whistle buoy is moored on the W side of a nasty rocky shoal, which you leave to the N when entering L'Abervrac'h via the Grand Chenal. Coming from

seaward, it is important to approach Le Libenter buoy from W of N and then to drop S of the buoy before heading into the estuary.

When approaching L'Abervrac'h from the Basse de Portsall in murky weather, the main danger lies in passing Le Libenter buoy without realizing it and then running on towards the shoal itself. But if, on Admiralty Chart No. 1432, you draw a line from Ile Vierge lighthouse through Le Libenter buoy towards Basse de Portsall, you will see that this represents a safe approach course to Le Libenter buoy of 074°T. So from Basse de Portsall, first make good due E true for 2¼ miles to put you on this 'glide path', and then make good 074°T for the 3 miles to Le Libenter buoy.

The advantage of this transit course is that you can keep checking the bearing of Ile Vierge RDF beacon to make sure you are on track. With a bit of luck, you should hear Le Libenter's whistle as you get close. However, if, having run your distance, you don't locate the buoy, the safest plan is to head back W for a couple of miles and then turn seawards into safe water.

Bad Weather *en route*

If, on passage from Plymouth to L'Abervrac'h, a favourable north-westerly backs to the SW and freshens, the best bet is usually to stay on the starboard tack and simply to carry on for the North Brittany coast. As you approach the land you will obtain some lee, and if the front is short-lived and the wind soon veers, you can follow it round and make westing again.

The Bay of Morlaix is a useful area to head for if the wind stays hard in the SW. The easiest shelter can be found in its NW corner at Port de Bloscon, just round the corner from Roscoff. There are some well-maintained local moorings a little way S of the

Ro-Ro terminal, and you will be protected here in any westerly weather.

If you can take the ground easily, Roscoff itself offers a pleasant berth and is conveniently placed for slipping out and heading W again when tide and weather serve. In reasonable visibility, you can carry the flood up the estuary for about 7 miles to Morlaix itself, with its sleepy locked basin and attractive old town. This is a congenial spot in which to wait for gales to die down, but it is easy to lose touch with the elements so far inland. 'Harbouritis' can set in and defer your progress towards L'Abervrac'h.

The Return Passage

The return trip to Plymouth involves a simpler landfall than the outward passage. The tides are much weaker on the English side of the Channel and you have the Eddystone lighthouse as a handy off-lying signpost. Given a north-westerly, there is much to be said for leaving L'Abervrac'h about 1 hour after local HW. You will then pick up a full 6 hours of powerful W-going stream which will improve your slant for Plymouth. A stiff north-easterly brings the most unpleasant conditions for this passage—you will be sailing hard on the wind and fighting a typically choppy easterly sea. Falmouth or Fowey give you a better slant, but it is preferable to delay your departure, phone the office, and relax in L'Abervrac'h until the wind eases or shifts!

Entering Plymouth at night is no problem, with Eddystone coming up first and the light on the W end of the breakwater leading you into the Sound. The entrance is wide and deep and can be safely approached in onshore gales, so long as you know more or less where you are. In fog, be sure to clear Eddystone by at least ½ mile and then start homing in on Penlee Point RDF beacon. The soundings will give you a good idea when you are within ¼ mile of the coast, and there is a fog horn (*10s*) situated at the end of the headland. From Penlee you can either set a course for the W end of Plymouth breakwater and pick up its fog bell (*15s*), or else feel your way round into Cawsand Bay and anchor.

High-speed Factors

If you average 15 knots, the passage from Plymouth breakwater to an off-shore waypoint 3 miles N of Le Libenter W-cardinal buoy should take about 7 hours. Your track will lead a couple of miles E of Eddystone before you strike out across the rather lonely stretch of sea at this Atlantic end of the English Channel. You can expect to meet the first of the up-Channel shipping about 50 miles out, and the total width of the traffic lanes will be something like 35 miles on the course you'll be steering.

This passage is a longish haul in open water, so it is not wise to set off unless you are pretty sure of a day of quiet conditions. Unlike the Dartmouth to Les Heaux crossing, you don't have the option of making for Guernsey if the wind freshens from the W or SW on the way. The only feasible alternative would be the Morlaix River which, although it involves no saving in distance, gives you an easier course if you wanted to take a south-westerly sea farther round on the starboard bow. A useful landfall waypoint for the Morlaix River is a position 2 miles N of Astan E-cardinal buoy, which lies close E of the Ile de Batz.

From the offshore waypoint 3 miles N of Le Libenter, aim to make good due S towards this buoy, but don't stray E of a line joining the waypoint and the buoy. As you approach Le Libenter, the coast to the SSW comes up well on radar, but the low-lying L'Abervrac'h estuary to the SE is more difficult to identify.

Pilot Books, etc.

Admiralty NP27, *The Channel Pilot.*

Admiralty NP74, *List of Lights, Vol. A.*

North Brittany Pilot, K. Adlard Coles and the RCC Pilotage Foundation, 5th edn (rev.) 1984, published by Adlard Coles.

French Pilot, vol. 1, M. Robson, 1983 edn, published by Nautical.

The Shell Pilot to the English Channel, J. Coote, vols 1 and 2, 1987 edns, published by Faber and Faber.

Channel Islands and North Brittany Cruising, P. Cumberlidge, 1st edn 1990, published by Yachting Monthly.

The Cruising Association Handbook, 7th edn 1990, published by the Cruising Association.

Adlard Coles Pilot Pack, Vol. 3, B. Goulder, 1st edn 1989, published by Adlard Coles.

Charts

Admiralty:

No. 2675—The English Channel

No. 1267—Falmouth to Plymouth

No. 1613—Eddystone Rocks to Berry Head

No. 1900—Approaches to Plymouth

No. 1901—Smeaton Pass and the Narrows

No. 1432—Le Four to Ile Vierge

Imray:

C6—Start Point to Lizard Point

C10—Western English Channel Passage Chart

C14—Plymouth harbours and rivers

C35—Bay of Morlaix to L'Aberildut

Stanford

No. 2—English Channel, Western Section

No. 13—Start Point to Land's End

No. 17—North Brittany Coast

Tidal Atlases

Stanford's Tidal Atlas, English Channel West (recommended).

Admiralty NP250, *English and Bristol Channels.*

Tidal Streams (times based on HW Dover)

Position	E-going stream starts	W-going stream starts
Off Plymouth	+0430	−0130
Off L'Abervrac'h (10 miles offshore)	+0200	−0400
Off L'Abervrac'h (close inshore)	HW	−0530

Tidal Differences and Heights

Place	Time of HW on Dover	MHWS	Heights above chart datum in metres		
			MLWS	MHWN	MLWN
Plymouth	−0535	5.5	0.8	4.4	2.2
Falmouth	−0605	5.3	0.6	4.2	1.9
Fowey	−0545	5.4	0.6	4.3	2.0
Salcombe	−0530	5.3	0.7	4.1	2.1
L'Abervrac'h (Ile Cézon)	+0550	8.0	1.1	6.1	2.9

Important Lights

English coast:

Eddystone Rocks (*Fl2, 10s, 24M, and FR vis 112°-129°T, 13M*); Plymouth Breakwater West End (*FLWR, 10s, 15M, 12M, and Iso4s vis 031°-039°T, 12M*); Lizard Point (*Fl3s, 29M*); Start Point (*Fl3, 10s, 25M*).

Brittany coast:

Ile Vierge (*Fl5s, 27M*); Créac'h light, Ushant (*Fl2, 10s, 33M*); Le Four (*Fl5, 15s, 20M*); Le Libenter buoy (*Q9, 15s*); L'Abervrac'h outer leading lights in line 100°T—front at Ile Vrac'h (*QR, 6M*), *rear* at Lanvaon (*QFl, intens 097°-104°T, 10M*); L'Abervrac'h inner dir. light bearing 128°T (*Oc2, WRG, 6s, 8-6M*).

RDF Beacons

English coast:

Penlee Point (*298.8kHz, 'PE', 50M, No. 1*); Lizard Point (*298.8kHz, 'LZ', 70M, No. 6*); Start Point (*298.8kHz, 'SP', 70M, No. 2*).

Brittany coast:

Ile Vierge (*298.8kHz, 'VG', 70M, No. 5*); Ushant, Pointe de Créac'h (*308.0kHz, 'CA', 100M, No. 6*).

Weather Forecasts (all times GMT except where otherwise stated)

BBC shipping forecast area:

Plymouth

VHF coast radio stations:

Start Point—0803, 2003, on Ch. 26
Pendennis—0803, 2003, on Ch. 62
Ouessant—0633, 1133, on Ch. 82
Le Conquet—0633, 1133, on Ch. 26

Marinecall:

0898 500 458

Local radio coastal forecasts:

BBC Radio Devon—shipping forecasts Mon-Fri at local times 0605, 0833, 1310, 1733; Sat at 0605, 0633, 0833, 1310; Sun at 0833, 1310. Plymouth frequencies: *855 kHz, 351m, 103.4 MHz FM*; ILR Plymouth (Plymouth Sound)—coastal forecasts, if available, at local times 0610, 0706, 0750, 0815, 1745, 2103, 2203, 2302, 2359. Frequencies: *1152 kHz, 261m, 97.0 MHz FM*

Met Office forecasts:

Plymouth Weather Centre, Tel. 0752 402534

11 ACROSS BISCAY

For yachtsmen who usually sail within easy reach of the Channel, the Bay of Biscay may represent a gently niggling challenge just beyond the normal run of summer cruises. Part of the attraction is that a passage across Biscay is really a miniature ocean voyage which can yet be undertaken within a fairly normal holiday period. There is also the lure of northern Spain, with its mountainous coast, dramatic rias and wild unspoilt anchorages.

If you are organized and not based too far N or E, it is possible to squeeze a return trip to Spain into three weeks, although this is a tighter timetable than most skippers would choose. Even for those moored near the Solent, simply getting down-Channel can take a while given a typical English summer. Having reached the tip of Brittany, you might linger for a day or two in some agreeable haven to carry out last-minute preparations, or wait for a depression to pass. Time slips by, and remember that you need to schedule 3–4 days each way for crossing the Bay.

When holiday weeks are precious, there is much to be said for a two-stage expedition, with one crew taking the boat out to somewhere like La Coruña and another bringing her back. This can help avoid a common problem experienced when crossing

Biscay: that when you eventually reach the N coast of Spain, it is time to turn round and come home again. To sail this far and miss out on the spectacular local cruising is indeed a terrible shame.

Of course, modern boats have the advantage of higher cruising speeds than were possible not so long ago. The rhumb line distance from the Raz de Sein to La Coruña is about 330 miles, and there is a significant difference between 3½ days at 4 knots and 2¼ days at 6 knots. We always used to reckon on 3 nights at sea if everything went according to plan, but a yacht of recent design with a free wind might only need to spend 2 nights out if she makes an early-morning start.

Boats leaving from Cornwall, Ireland or the Bristol Channel may opt for a single long haul, keeping outside Ushant and barely sighting France before striking out across the Bay. If you are coming down the English Channel, though, it is more usual to make for L'Abervrac'h first, slip 'round the corner' to Camaret or perhaps Audierne, and then wait for a suitable patch of weather before setting off into open water.

I will adopt such a strategy here, starting the passage planning from L'Abervrac'h. Although L'Abervrac'h is a delightfully sleepy Brittany estu-

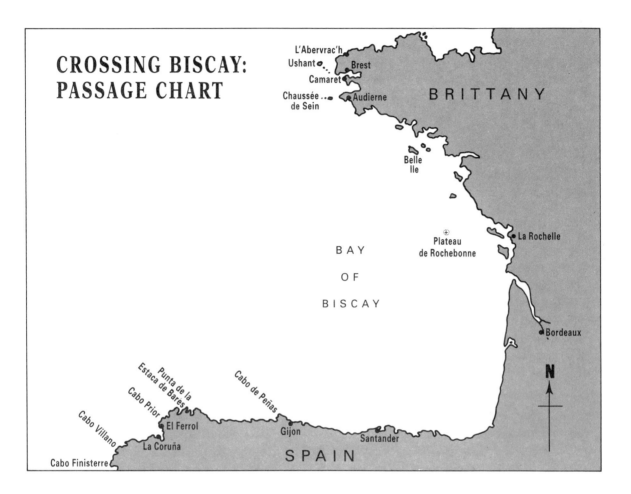

CROSSING BISCAY: PASSAGE CHART

ary, it always seems to have the exciting atmosphere of a cruising crossroads. Boats that are outward bound meet boats coming home, and their skippers visit each other to spend long hours poring over charts, pilot books and weather maps.

The Chenal du Four

This well-marked passage leads between the W coast of the Brest peninsula and the off-lying islands of Ushant, Molène, Quéménés and Béniguet, providing the most common route for yachts bound between the English Channel and the Bay of Biscay. The Chenal du Four is wider than it appears on a small-scale chart and is quite straightforward in reasonable visibility, by day or night, so long as you carry the stream in your favour.

You often meet a somewhat forbidding Atlantic swell in the N approaches between L'Abervrac'h and Le Four lighthouse, but farther S you obtain some shelter from the islands and the swell usually dies down. However, this S part of the channel, between Pointe de Corsen and Pointe de St Mathieu, can be choppy in a fresh wind against tide.

It is best to leave L'Abervrac'h 1 hour or so before local HW. From Le Libenter W-cardinal entrance

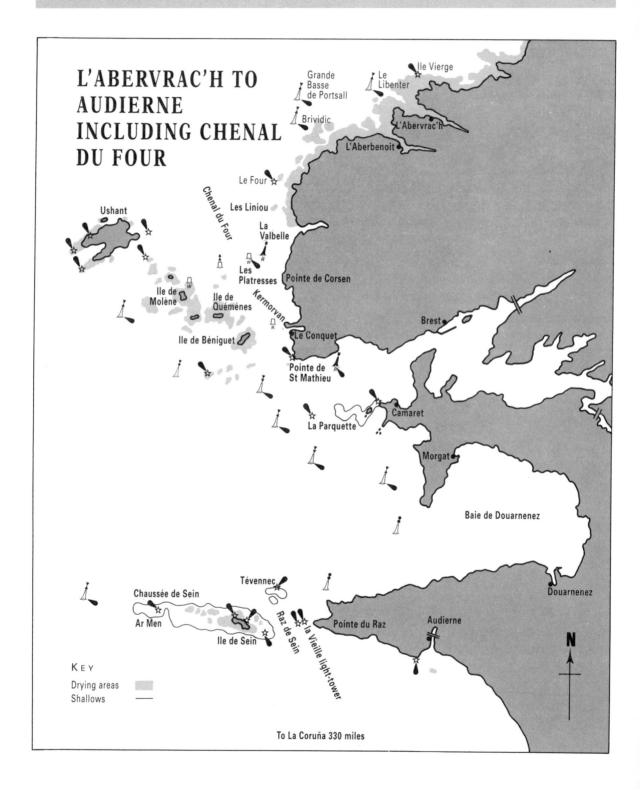

L'ABERVRAC'H TO AUDIERNE INCLUDING CHENAL DU FOUR

Grande Basse de Portsall

Brividic

Le Libenter

Ile Vierge

L'Abervrac'h

L'Aberbenoît

Le Four

Chenal du Four

Les Liniou

Ushant

La Valbelle

Les Platresses

Pointe de Corsen

Ile de Molène

Ile de Quéménes

Kermorvan

Ile de Béniguet

Le Conquet

Brest

Pointe de St Mathieu

La Parquette

Camaret

Morgat

Baie de Douarnenez

Tévennec

Chaussée de Sein

Ar Men

Ile de Sein

Raz de Sein

La Vieille light-tower

Pointe du Raz

Audierne

Douarnenez

KEY

Drying areas

Shallows

N

To La Coruña 330 miles

buoy, make good 260°T for 5 miles towards Grande Basse de Portsall W-cardinal buoy, the corner-mark for this stretch of coast. You'll be stemming the last of the flood on this leg, but should be well placed to catch most of the fair stream in the Four. You needn't round Portsall buoy, but it is wise to come within ½ mile of it before turning SSW to pass outside Brividic W-cardinal buoy, which lies 1½ miles S of Grande Basse de Portsall.

From Brividic buoy, make good 205°T for 4 miles to pass a good ½ mile W of Le Four lighthouse, a gaunt stone tower which stands about 1 mile off the mainland coast. Don't cut this mark any closer because there is a plateau of dangers not far to the NE. Once past Le Four, make good 190°T to leave Les Liniou, a distinctive string of above-water rocks, about ¾ mile to port. Staying on this course for 3 miles beyond Les Liniou, you come to the gate-way for the S part of the Chenal du Four—La Valbelle red pillar buoy left close to port and Les Plâtresses white tower to starboard.

The leading marks for this part of the Four Chan-nel are the two lighthouses of Kermorvan and Pointe de St Mathieu in transit bearing 158°T. This line is useful at night, but I have never found it either necessary or easy to pick out during the day, when it is simpler to follow the buoys SSE and then S down the fairway. If you are working against the wind, you can tack outside the buoys to gain ground so long as you refer carefully to Admiralty Chart No. 3345.

When under sail, though, keep a close eye on time and tide. You should try to reach Pointe de St Mathieu before the new flood starts coming back because the streams are strong in the shallow S part of the Chenal du Four. Le Conquet is a useful bolt-hole if you find yourself running late.

Having cleared Pointe de St Mathieu, you are faced with a choice: (a) to turn ESE for Camaret

and wait there until you are ready to set off across the Bay; to continue south for Audierne via the Raz de Sein, with the same object in mind; or (b) to put to sea straightaway if the weather pattern looks set-tled, either via the Raz or passing outside Chaussée de Sein W-cardinal buoy.

It all depends on the weather, your state of readi-ness and how you and your crew feel. If you are keen to reach Spain and conditions look reason-able, there is much to be said for getting to sea sooner rather than later. Once you become 'harbourized', there is always a certain inertia to overcome in deciding when to leave again, especi-ally for a 3-day passage. If, on the other hand, the met chart looks a bit unsettled, it makes sense to tuck in somewhere to avoid being caught out by a wayward depression.

As a place to rest up and wait for a favourable wind, Audierne now has certain advantages over Camaret. Although Camaret is a very pleasant spot with a snug harbour, the yacht berths are a consid-erable walk from the town, which makes shopping hard work if you are laying in stores for a Biscay passage. However, Audierne's new pontoons are right next to the square, with shops and cafes close at hand and a large supermarket not far away. Christel, the helpful and attractive *maîtresse du port*, will keep you posted with forecasts while you are pondering when to leave.

Although you can only enter or leave Audierne near HW, the going is clear once you have put to sea. Departing from Camaret, you still have to nego-tiate the Chaussée de Sein, either via the Raz, which means catching the tide, or by working well off-shore. Leaving from Audierne, you shave about 18 miles off the passage to La Coruña; this may not seem a lot in 330 miles, but it might just save a night at sea and gain you an extra day in Spain.

The Raz de Sein is temperamental and can produce savage overfalls with even a moderate wind against the tide. The passage is best taken at dead slack water, just as the stream is about to flow in your favour. Coming from the N, you should aim to be 1½ miles due E of Tévennec islet half an hour before HW Brest. Coming from the S on the return trip, you should be 1½ miles S by E of la Vieille light-tower at 5½ hours after HW Brest.

Choosing Your Time

Your overall timetable will probably have been worked out at leisure, when you were armchair cruising during winter evenings in front of the fire. The Admiralty *Bay of Biscay Pilot* makes good reading for planning purposes, with the proviso that its long-run statistics do not necessarily forecast the weather for any particular year. In the past, May, June and July have shown the highest percentage of north-westerlies in the Bay, while August tends to bring westerly or south-westerly winds.

June and July have the lowest average frequency of gales and strong winds. Poor visibility at sea during the summer seems to be most common in July, although the more exposed coast stations in N Spain experience the highest number of foggy days in May or June.

When making a Biscay passage as part of a holiday cruise, I have usually opted to leave Dartmouth in the second half of June and be cruising Spanish waters in July, thereby hoping to minimize the risk of gales. Even with a crew change and 3 weeks each, the return trip is then made in early August, when any south-westerlies are a help rather than a hindrance. Within that broad framework you might, for the outward leg, prefer neap tides for navigating the North Brittany coast, the Chenal du Four and the Raz de Sein.

Having finally arrived at Camaret or Audierne, most skippers would like to see a settled spell of fine weather and moderate winds from a northerly quarter. An established Azores high is usually good news, perhaps giving you some steady northwesterlies, although if the ridge extends too strongly into the Western Approaches you are likely to experience a shortage of wind instead of a surfeit. A stable period of easterlies or north-easterlies can be helpful, such as you might obtain from the bottom edge of a high centred over Britain.

What you don't want is a procession of lows marching in from the Atlantic, with their fronts swinging across Biscay. If you are dealt this kind of unsettled hand, the problem is to judge how far S the influence of these depressions might stretch. Listening to summer shipping forecasts, you often find that sea area Biscay is less prone to severe conditions than Sole or Plymouth, but of course the Bay is susceptible to swell from heavy weather anywhere in the offing; and while Force 5 or 6 may be more acceptable than the gales or near gales farther N, it still represents a good deal of wind in the open sea.

It is not only freshening weather than can cause problems. If the wind should back between W and S once you have set off, it can increase your passage distance significantly, or force you much farther into the Bay than intended. For this reason, even if you are making for La Coruña, it is prudent to be well provided with charts for at least as far E as Santander; it may be better to switch your destination than endure a long slog to windward.

Unfortunately, if the weather remains unco-operative while you are waiting in Brittany, there is nothing much to be gained by cruising farther down the coast. You are simply swinging around a more or less constant radius from NW Spain and giving yourself a worse slant in the event of westerly winds.

On Passage

Having set off across Biscay 'towards' La Coruña, a navigator has to decide how far to stand offshore as a hedge against being forced into the Bay if the wind should back and freshen halfway across. This question may be difficult to resolve in practice. Given the usual mix of summer weather, you can sometimes lose as much by chasing westing in anticipation as by being forced E when the elements decide to misbehave.

If you are expecting gales or near-gales, it makes sense to gain searoom to windward. But in moderate conditions, you will probably build in enough offing by working to a track which terminatēs about 20–30 miles NW of the entrance of La Coruña. Allowing for a bit of extra leeway, some unpredicted surface drift and the wind heading you for a while as it always seems to, you are likely to end up within reach of the landfall stretch of coast, somewhere between Cabo Ortegal and Islas Sisargas.

The Biscay tidal streams are only of practical significance close inshore. Drawing away from the Brittany coast, you begin to experience currents of a more oceanic nature. The direction and rate of these drifts vary considerably, but you are likely to meet a broadly ESE set in the N part of the Bay and a westerly set near the Spanish coast. These two components often seem to cancel each other out on a passage across to La Coruña.

However, the surface currents experienced at any given time are influenced by the wind recently prevailing in the Bay and the Atlantic approaches. Assessing these currents during a passage is largely a matter of supplementing the information in the pilot books with intelligent guesswork. Glancing back through my logs recently, I discovered that in moderate W or north-westerly weather, I have usually allowed for an ESE set of about 10 miles a day for most of the crossing. In sustained easterlies or north-easterlies, I've tended to disregarded the current.

Whatever your initial plan, it is prudent to monitor the apparent set as far as possible, either with sights whenever you can catch the sun, or by using RDF, Decca or Sat-nav. Having estimated this set for the first part of the crossing, be on your guard for a change in the current as you approach the Spanish coast.

RDF bearings are useful for this purpose for about the first 24 hours at sea and again within 100 miles of your landfall. On the Brittany side, the best beacons are Ile de Sein lighthouse (*303.4kHz, 'SN', 70M*), Penmarc'h (*289.6kHz, 'UH', 50M*) and Belle Ile (*303.4kHz, 'BT', 100M*). The most strategically placed Spanish beacon is Estaca de Bares (*301.1kHz, 'BA', 100M*), which can be crossed with Cabo Villano (*310.3kHz, 'VI', 100M*) or Cabo de Peñas (*301.1kHz, 'PS', 50M*), depending on which side of it you end up.

Decca and Sat-nav

There is a dead area for Decca near the middle of the Bay of Biscay, especially at night, when you run out of clear range of the SW British chain before picking up the NW Spanish chain. The French chain is not much help on this offshore passage, because its stations are well inland and the master is always farther away than either the SW British or the NW Spanish.

A Sat-nav makes an ideal companion in the open waters of Biscay, where there is no problem about waiting even a few hours for a good satellite pass. When a satellite does come over, the signal is usually strong and reliable and the resulting fix more accurate than one obtained from fading Decca transmissions.

Heavy Weather on Passage

If you are caught by heavy weather halfway across Biscay, there is no option but to take it on the chin. You therefore need to be confident that your boat and crew can cope with whatever adverse conditions might come your way. Provided you are well offshore when the going gets rough, the seas will at least be long and regular and you'll have plenty of room under your lee. Beware of being caught near the edge of the Continental Shelf in westerly gales, because the sudden shoaling from oceanic depths can cause very confused seas locally.

The Landfall

Landfalls are always exciting, but a landfall on N Spain seems to conjure up a special aura of mystery. The country behind the shoreline is remote, mountainous and sparsely populated. In clear visibility you can sometimes see the inland peaks from 50 miles off, long before the cliffs lift above the horizon. If you were bound for La Coruña and all has gone according to plan, you should be approaching the Galician coast somewhere between Cabo Ortegal and Isla Sisargas, a NW facing stretch about 50 miles long.

Cabo Ortegal is an impressive headland which juts into the Bay of Biscay some 30 miles NE of La Coruña. Close behind the cliffs, several peaks rise almost sheer to 2000 feet—Garita del Limo, Garita de Herbeira and Monte Miranda. For many yachtsmen coming from England or Brittany, these mountains will be the first glimpse of Spain after a longish spell at sea. Punta Candelaria lies about 8 miles WSW of Cape Ortegal and its light is usually a welcome sight if you are making for La Coruña.

Although this coast is steep-to with few off-lying dangers, it needs treating with respect in strong onshore winds, when a powerful swell rolls in from the Atlantic. Out in deep water the seas are predictable, even during gales, but the soundings reduce suddenly within 25 miles of Cabo Ortegal.

If you are unlucky enough to meet heavy westerly weather towards the end of a Biscay passage, you will usually be safer staying offshore until things quieten down, rather than running in to make a landfall. An additional danger is that low cloud and rain can obscure the high headlands and their lights, even when visibility is apparently clear at sea level.

Close W of Punta Candelaria is the entrance to Ria de Cedeira, worth bearing in mind as an overnight stop if you have made your landfall a bit further E than anticipated. Keep to the E side when entering Ria de Cedeira and then turn to port to anchor behind the breakwater.

If the weather dictates a landfall to the E of Cabo Ortegal, there is a good anchorage at the head of Ria del Barquero, right in the SE corner off Vicedo village. Barquero is useful in heavy westerly weather because Punta de la Estaca de Bares provides some lee from this direction before you reach the entrance to the Ria. Barquero is also a possible retreat if you meet fog; the coast here is steep-to and in calm conditions you can safely home on to Estaca de Bares RDF beacon and pick your way into the Ria.

Twelve miles SW of Cedeira is Cabo Prior, with its prominent conical hill and powerful lighthouse. Once you have rounded this point, La Coruña is only 12 miles away, but it is wise to avoid three shoal areas—Bajos Torracidos, Bajo Cabaleiro and Banco de las Laixinas—if the onshore swell is at all heavy.

LANDFALL FOR LA CORUÑA

La Coruña

The port of La Coruña lies on the W side of Ria de la Coruña, whose W extremity is the low promontory of Punta Herminio. Torre de Hércules, a conspicuous square lighthouse, stands 1 mile or so N of the city near the end of Punta Herminio. Entering the Ria is straightforward, although you should avoid Banco Yacentes in fresh onshore winds or whenever there's a swell running.

The easiest approach is to keep Torre de Hércules bearing between S and SE until the two white octagonal towers on Punta de Mera come into line bearing 108°T. Follow this transit between Banco Yacentes and Punta Herminio, leave the green conical buoy off Punta Pragueira close to starboard, and then head S by E to round the main breakwater and enter the harbour. At the root of the breakwater you will find the friendly marina run by the Club

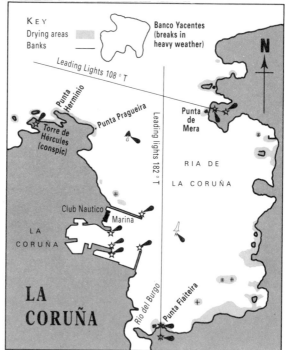

Nautico. Here you can look forward to a sheltered berth, a comfortable clubhouse and excellent showers. There is water at the pontoons and a fuelling point on the quay.

Changing Crews

La Coruña makes a good base for changing crews and there are three options for travelling by public transport:

1 The Plymouth to Santander ferry.
2 By rail via Paris and the border town of Hendaye.
3 By air via Santiago airport.

If you opt for the Santander ferry, you can either drive or take a train between Santander and La Coruña. If you drive, be sure to inform the ferry company that the car will be returning with a different party of passengers. The rail journey across France is surprisingly quick. There is a good overnight train from La Coruña central station which gets to Hendaye at breakfast time. From here you catch an express to Paris, arriving in the late afternoon, and thence to whichever ferry port you prefer.

Santiago airport is about 1 hour by road from La Coruña and an airport coach runs from the Hotel Atlantico. There are only one or two flights direct to London each week, although you can travel any day via Madrid. I have used the Madrid route when in a hurry, but it is expensive because you travel on two separate scheduled flights.

High-speed Factors

The 350-mile haul from Brittany across the Bay of Biscay to La Coruña is rarely undertaken by high-speed motor yachts, except on delivery trips. This is partly because this length of passage does not fall within the safe cruising range of most production boats, but also because Biscay should really be regarded as an ocean passage in miniature and, as such, is not usually reckoned to be the place for relatively light-displacement planing hulls.

Trying to predict fuel consumption can be a tricky business, but it is vital to err on the safe side if you are out in open water, allowing for reductions in speed made good because of adverse weather. As an example, a Birchwood 44 with twin Caterpillar 375 hp diesels might do 26–28 knots in reasonably calm water, when she will burn about 20 gallons per hour. The normal fuel capacity is 400 gallons, so you would have 20 hours to play with as an absolute maximum, with 17–18 hours being a more realistic limit. At 26 knots you'd cover 350 miles in 13½ hours, leaving you only 3½–4½ hours in reserve.

Boats on delivery often carry three 40-gallon drums of diesel lashed in the cockpit, which gives an extra 6 hours—another 150–170 miles—in calm water. Bear in mind, though, that it is by no means easy to transfer fuel at sea, and the drums have to very securely lashed.

The sheer size of the Bay of Biscay, and the fact that the weather patterns over Brittany and NW Spain are somewhat different, mean that you cannot guarantee that a calm settled spell with which you set out will hold right across the Bay. It must be said that, to some extent, a direct Biscay crossing in a high-speed boat has an element of gambling about it, a feature not normally considered a sound basis for seamanship.

It is generally safer and more interesting to reach La Coruña by a series of legs round the Biscay coast. Making the trip for pleasure, I would first cross the Channel to L'Abervrac'h and then hop round to Morgat, where there is a good marina and fuelling berth. From Morgat, the legs you choose are partly a matter of the kind of places you like visiting, but they will also depend on the easy availability of fuel.

Some useful and reasonably spaced fuel stops on the French coast are Lorient, L'Herbaudière Marina at the north tip of Ile de Noirmoutier, La Rochelle and Royan. The leg from La Rochelle to Royan is quite short, but it enables you to set off from Royan with full tanks for a longish day passage across the inner part of the Bay to Santander, a distance of about 180 miles. From Santander you can make an 85-mile leg along the N Spanish coast to Gijon, where you can get diesel at the root of the jetty. Gijon to La Coruña is then about 140 miles.

The N coast of Spain must not be underestimated, however. Even in settled weather, the long Atlantic swell is a reminder that you are cruising in large-scale oceanic waters, whose mood can change surprisingly quickly. It can often be an advantage to make coastal passages early in the morning during fine summer spells, aiming to arrive at your destination before midday. This is to avoid the unwelcome chop that onshore breezes can set up in the afternoon.

The harbours are well spaced and some can be difficult to enter in fresh onshore winds. You should carry Robin Brandon's *South Biscay Pilot* on board and there are now some excellent large-scale Admiralty charts for the N coast of Spain; if you are making the passage from Royan via Santander, it is worth carrying Nos. 74, 75, 78, 1133, 1155 and 1114. The whole of this high coast shows up well on radar, although from some distance offshore you can sometimes pick up the mountains behind the shoreline first.

Pilot Books, etc.

Admiralty NP27, *The Channel Pilot.*

Admiralty NP22, *Bay of Biscay Pilot.*

Admiralty NP67, *West Coasts of Spain and Portugal Pilot.*

Admiralty NP74, *List of Lights, Vol. A.*

Admiralty NP77, *List of Lights, Vol. D.*

North Brittany Pilot, K. Adlard Coles and the RCC Pilotage foundation, 5th edn (rev.) 1984, published by Adlard Coles.

North Biscay Pilot, RCC Pilotage Foundation, 4th edn (rev.) 1990, published by Adlard Coles.

South Biscay Pilot, R. Brandon, 3rd edn (rev.) 1987, published by Adlard Coles.

Admiralty Charts

No 1432—Le Four to Ile Vierge

No. 3345—Chenal du Four

No. 2643—Raz de Sein to Goulven, including Brest and Ushant

No. 798—Pointe de St Mathieu to Chaussée de Sein

No. 2351—Anse de Bénodet to Chaussée de Sein

No. 1104—Bay of Biscay

No. 1111—Punta de la Estaca de Bares to Cabo Toriñana

No. 1108—Gijon to Punta Candelaria

No. 1105—Santander to Gijon

No. 1122—Ports on the North Coast of Spain

No. 1114—Rias de Ares, Betanzos and La Coruña

Tidal Atlases

Stanford's Tidal Atlas, English Channel West (recommended).

Admiralty NP265, *France, West Coast.*

Tidal Streams (times based on HW Dover)

Position	N-going stream starts	S-going stream starts
Basse de Portsall buoy	+0030	+0545
Off Pointe de St Mathieu	−0045	+0530
Raz de Sein, off La Vieille	−0115	+0500

Tidal Differences and Heights

| Place | Time of HW on Dover | MHWS | Heights above chart datum in metres | | |
			MLWS	MHWN	MLWN
L'Abervrac'h	+0550	7.9	1.0	6.0	2.9
Le Conquet	+0530	7.1	1.3	5.5	2.9
Camaret	+0510	6.9	1.2	5.3	2.8
Audierne	+0455	5.2	0.8	3.9	2.0

| Place | Time of HW on Pointe de Grave | MHWS | Heights above chart datum in metres | | |
			MLWS	MHWN	MLWN
Ria del Barquero	−0035	3.9	0.4	3.0	1.4
Ria de Cedeira	−0040	3.8	0.4	2.9	1.3
La Coruña	−0110	3.6	0.5	2.8	1.3

Important Lights

Brittany coast:

Le Four (*Fl5, 15s, 20M*); Ushant, Le Stiff (*Fl2R, 20s, 25M*); Ushant, Créac'h (*Fl2, 10s, 33M*); Kermorvan (*Fl, 5s, 23M*); Pointe de St Mathieu (*Fl, 15s, 30M*); Ile de Sein, NW light (*Fl4, 25s, 31M*); Chaussée de Sein, Ar Men (*Fl3, 20s, 23M*); Tévennec (*QWR, 9M, 6M*); La Vieille (*Oc2+1, WRG, 12s, 15M, 12M, 11M*); La Plate (*VQ9, 10s, 8M*); Penmarc'h, Eckmühl (*Fl, 5s, 26M*); Penmarc'h, Menhir (*Oc2, WG, 6s, 8M, 4M*).

NW Spanish coast:

Punta de la Estaca de Bares (*Fl2, 7½s, 35M*); Punta Candelaria (*Fl, 3+1, 24s, 22M*); Cabo Prior (*Fl, 1+2, 15s, 34M*); Cabo Priorino Chico (*Fl, 5s, 11M*); Torre de Hércules (*Fl4, 20s, 32M*); Punta de Mera leading lights— *front* (*FR, 8M*), *rear* (*Oc2, 10s, 8M*); Islas Sisargas (*Fl3, 15s, 33M*); Cabo Villano (*Fl2, 15s, 40M*).

RDF Beacons

Brittany coast:

Ile Vierge (*298.8, 'VG', 70M, No. 5*); Ushant, Créac'h (*308, 'CA', 100M, No. 6*); Pointe de St Mathieu (*289.6, 'SM', 20M, No. 3*); Ile de Sein, NW light (*303.4, 'SN', 70M, No. 3*); Pointe de Penmarc'h, Eckmühl (*289.6, 'UH', 50M, No. 1*); Belle Ile (*303.4, 'BT', 100M, No. 2*).

NW Spanish coast:

Cabo de Peñas (*301.1, 'PS', 50M, Nos. 3, 4*); Asturias aero beacon (*325, 'AVS', 60M, cont.*); Estaca de Bares (*301.1, 'BA', 100M, Nos. 5, 6*); Cabo Priorino Chico (*305.7, 'C', 50M, Nos. 2, 4, 6*); Torre de Hércules (*305.7, 'L', 30M, Nos. 1, 3, 5*); La Coruña aero beacon (*401, 'LRA', 40M, cont.*); Cabo Villano (*310.3, 'VI', 100M, Nos. 1, 2*).

Weather Forecasts (all times GMT except where otherwise stated)

BBC shipping forecast areas:

   Plymouth, Biscay, Finisterre

VHF coast radio stations:

   Ouessant—0633, 1133, on Ch. 82

   Le Conquet—0633, 1133, on Ch. 26

   Pont l'Abbé—0633, 1133, on Ch. 27

   Belle Ile—0633, 1133, on Ch. 87

   Santander/Cabo de Peñas—1103, 1733, in Spanish only on VHF Ch. 26 or 1757.5 kHz

   La Coruña (Elris)—1103, 1733, in Spanish only on VHF Ch. 26 or 1748 kHz

Met Office forecasts:

   Useful overall view can be obtained from Plymouth Weather Centre, Tel. 0752 402534

12 FALMOUTH TO FASTNET

A crossing of the Celtic Sea from Cornwall to the S coast of Ireland is not, on the whole, to be undertaken lightly. Given a favourable slant, the shortest open passage you can get away with is about 140 miles, from Land's End to Crosshaven perhaps, or nearby Kinsale. If you head farther W towards the Fastnet Rock and the attractive cruising area of Long Island Bay, it will cost you more like 170 miles in a direction largely contrary to the prevailing winds.

Many yachtsmen experience an understandable kind of inertia when planning a cruise to Ireland. For the same longish distances involved, you could be well on your way across the Bay of Biscay bound for the rias of NW Spain, a decidedly warmer sun, and some robust local wine. Or you could already be snugly anchored in one of the South Brittany rivers, enjoying lunch in the style to which only the French seem accustomed.

It therefore takes a conscious effort of will to turn N round Land's End and strike out across a somewhat notorious stretch of water in search of the country where, so they say, if it's not already raining it is just about to, and where the cost of a bottle of almost anything will make you wince. Yet the effort is undoubtedly worthwhile. The wild, indented coast of Ireland's SW tip offers some memorable cruising and a sense of solitude that is becoming increasingly rare.

July is a good month for making the outward passage. You stand a reasonable chance of picking up a spell of settled weather and, if you can possibly arrange it, a few days of easterlies. Falmouth is a useful port of departure, where you can attend to any last-minute preparations and wait for a fair wind. The main haul from, say, 5 miles N of the Seven Stones light-ship to the Fastnet Rock, involves making good about 300°T for not quite 155 miles—hard-going in a north-westerly but pleasant sailing in a moderate breeze from anywhere E. A south-westerly is satisfactory, but a wind from this quarter usually seems to be either too strong or short-lived.

Weather apart, there are few complications once you have cleared the shipping and strongish tides around the Lizard and Land's End. The streams right out in the Celtic Sea are weak and you normally meet little in the way of traffic. In some respects, making a landfall anywhere along Ireland's S shore is relatively straightforward; much easier, for example, than approaching North Brittany.

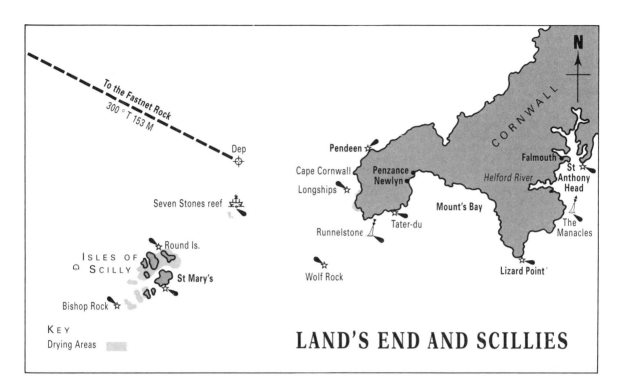

LAND'S END AND SCILLIES

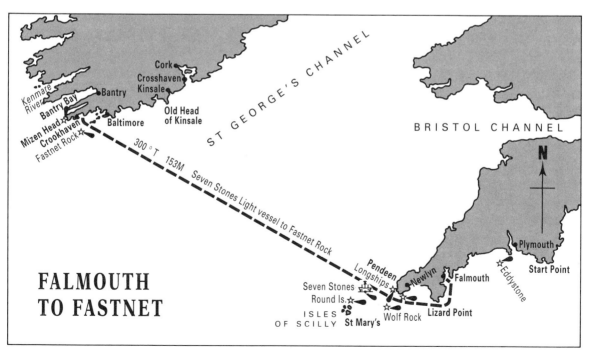

FALMOUTH TO FASTNET

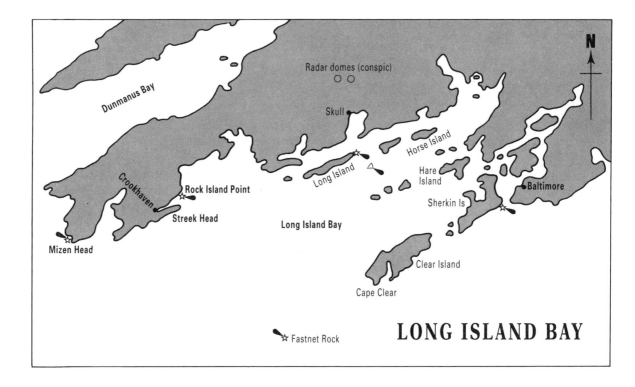

LONG ISLAND BAY

The coast is high and steep-to, and there are practically no off-lying dangers. The tidal streams are generally moderate inshore, with only a handful of local patches where rates reach 2–3 knots. The spring range is not quite 3 m in the region of Long Island Bay and about 3½ m farther E near Cork.

However, by English Channel standards, lights and RDF beacons are sparse. For nearly 60 miles W from the entrance to Cork Harbour, there are but two principal lighthouses—the Old Head of Kinsale and Galley Head—until you reach Fastnet itself. In effect, only two RDF beacons cover the same length of coast: the Old Head itself (296.5kHz, 'OH', 50M, No. 2) and Mizen Head (*308kHz, 'MZ', 100M, No. 4*), 9 miles NW of Fastnet. Ballycotton Island beacon (*296.5kHz, 'BN', 50M, No. 1*), 10 miles E of Cork harbour entrance, transmits on the same cycle as the Old Head.

Because the navigation aids are few and far between, and also because of the numerous unlit fishing nets laid some way offshore, it is prudent to avoid closing the land at night, especially with indifferent visibility. In fact there is much to be said for the once traditional pattern of landfall—aiming to arrive a safe distance off at night, so that you can hope to identify at least two lights and confirm your position, but not approaching the coast until after dawn. You then have the whole day in front of you for finding your way into somewhere safe.

A Passage via the Isles of Scilly?

Making for Fastnet by way of the Isles of Scilly is an attractive option if you have time. It adds a few miles to the overall trip, but cuts down the open sea leg to 150 miles and gives a slightly better slant in westerly weather.

The trouble with calling at the Scillies is that they are such a compelling cruising ground that you can have difficulty tearing yourself away and heading seaward again! If you do have strong will-power, the handiest anchorage for departure is New Grimsby Harbour between Tresco and Bryher. From here it is easy to slip out northwards at any state of tide.

Returning from Fastnet via the Scillies is less advisable than calling there on the way out, because making a safe landfall on these low-lying islands from the N and W requires accurate navigation and good visibility. The considerable number of wrecks that litter the archipelago are a testament to its power to lure seafarers into danger, and I must admit that I like to see the long red flash of Round Island light well away to the S when coming back from Ireland.

A Sample Passage

Suppose you are comfortably holed up in Falmouth, waiting for the all-important green light from the met office. You will be looking for a fairly settled period of weather and a forecast in which you can see nothing nasty for a good three days ahead. Some moderate easterlies or north-easterlies would do the job nicely, so a slow-moving ridge of high pressure out to the W and slack, not too low pressure over Europe, would supply the kind of conditions you want.

If the pattern is such that you are getting a classic series of depressions moving in from the Atlantic and tracking across the West Country, your luck is probably out for Ireland unless you are prepared simply to set off and take the rough with the smooth. If this picture looked like continuing, though, I'd be tempted to pick a 24-hour window and head across to Brittany!

It is over 55 miles from Falmouth round Lizard Point to a convenient departure position about 5 miles due N of the Seven Stones light-ship. Depending on wind and tide, it is best if you can leave Falmouth in the day, to be sure of clearing the Land's End shipping lanes before dark. Newlyn or Penzance are possible bolt-holes if the weather should deteriorate in the early stages of the passage.

The tide round the Lizard is an important consideration. If possible, choose a period for setting off in which local HW is around 0500 and then leave Falmouth something like 2 hours *after* high, that is, at about 4 hours *before* HW Dover. Assuming an average cruising speed of 5 knots, you will find the stream running steadily in your favour by the time you reach the Lizard. You can then carry the Channel ebb right across Mount's Bay to the Runnel Stone buoy, picking up the N-going stream off the Longships. Aim to pass at least 1 mile seaward of the Longships and make for a position 5 miles or so W of Cape Cornwall.

You will now be on the inshore edge of the N-going shipping lane in the Land's End separation scheme. From here, it is preferable to head due W to cross the lanes at right angles. The tide will be setting you N, away from the Seven Stones reef, and you should end up somewhere between 5 and 8 miles due N of the light-ship (*Fl3, 30s, 25M*) no later than 6 hours after HW Dover. The stream will be S-going in another couple of hours.

If the wind does not allow you to set off on the direct course of about 300°T, make due allowance for this southerly set when deciding which tack to start on. It is a good idea to get well clear of the Seven Stones and the Isles of Scilly at an early stage. As you draw beyond the Scillies, you'll probably meet some shipping bound to or from the outer separation scheme, which lies between 10 and 20 miles W of the islands. Once you have left this traffic astern, you should only come across the occasional ship until you start approaching the Irish coast.

The tactics you adopt on passage will depend largely on the prevailing weather and what you make of the forecast. If you are unlucky enough to be headed by a north-westerly, alternate tacks of 20 miles or so are probably a safe bet, but you could perhaps think in terms of a landfall in the vicinity of Kinsale rather than flogging all the way out to Fastnet. In this case, take note of the gas rigs which lie 25 miles SE of the Old Head of Kinsale.

As you draw within 10–15 miles of the Fastnet Rock, you may encounter shipping using the Fastnet separation scheme. The Rock itself is sheer and can be passed reasonably close-to. The famous, whitewashed lighthouse makes a striking sight and the hills of County Cork are now tantalizingly close. This is a hard moment for the race crews, who have to be content with a brief glimpse of the shore as they tack round the lighthouse and set off south-westward again into the empty wastes of the Celtic Sea.

From the Fastnet, the easiest haven to make for is usually Crookhaven, just over 6 miles to the NW. This long natural inlet is entered close S of Rock Island Point and can provide good shelter from all quarters. Crookhaven's restful anchorage is just the place to unwind after a passage, while you gently make or renew your acquaintance with Ireland. The village and quay lie on the S side of the harbour and both the small general store and O'Sullivan's bar are delightfully welcoming in their own ways.

Bad Weather on Passage

Memories of historic Fastnet Race gales in early August tend to make one naturally uneasy about the weather during this crossing. Yet it is interesting to recall one of the observations from the 1979 Race Inquiry, that 'there have been a number of races sailed in gale force winds, but light to moderate weather predominated in races sailed between 1963 and 1977'.

Probably the best advice is not to leave the safety of Cornwall until you are reasonably sure of the weather. If you *are* caught out, say in a rising westerly or south-westerly, much depends on how far across you've managed to get before being forced to take action. Provided you are well on your way and conditions are stiff rather than severe, you have the option of coming off the wind and making for Cork harbour or Kinsale. Cork is the safer refuge, being accessible in practically all weathers, but the entrance to Kinsale is partly sheltered by the Old Head and is satisfactory if there is not too much S in the wind.

The coast in the vicinity of Fastnet is not an easy landfall in poor visibility, when the safest plan is to stay at sea. Farther E it is possible, in calm murky conditions, to home in on the Old Head RDF beacon and then use the sharp null of the back-bearing to find your way into Kinsale.

The Return Passage

The homeward trip from Fastnet to Falmouth is usually easier than the outward passage because the prevailing winds are more or less behind you. I avoid calling at the Scillies unless the weather is settled and the visibility good, but the powerful RDF beacon on Round Island (*308kHz, 'RR', 100M, No. 5*) is invaluable as you approach the end of Cornwall. Land's End aero beacon (*114.4kHz, 'LND', cont.*) is useful once you draw E of Round Island.

High-speed Factors

Few motor boats seem to find their way to the SW coast of Ireland. To some extent this is understandable, when you consider the warmer, sunnier attractions to be had farther south. Yet the dramatically indented coast between Baltimore and the Kenmare River is good motor-boating country. The fjords themselves are comparatively sheltered, although you sometimes need to change anchorages in a hurry if the wind suddenly shifts. The passages between the inlets can be rough-going in fresh weather, but a fast power boat can take advantage of a quiet spell to hop from Crookhaven to Dunmanus, say, or from Bantry Bay to Kenmare.

Not many motor-boat skippers would consider the direct passage from Falmouth to Crookhaven, a total distance of about 230 miles. The length of the passage, as such, is not usually the most daunting factor. If you can average 20 knots, your passage time will be about 12 hours, so you can expect to complete the trip in daylight if you make an early start and all goes well. It is really the psychological aspect that tends to be the most significant. The Celtic Sea feels a lonely stretch of water and once you are off the tip of Cornwall in the vicinity of Land's End, to take a departure for the distant Fastnet Rock feels as though you are setting off towards the edge of the world. By contrast, a crossing of the English Channel down to L'Abervrac'h seems like quite a friendly and light-hearted undertaking.

You can overcome this problem in two ways. One is to take the coast-hopping route, making short legs between Falmouth, Newlyn, Padstow, Milford Haven, Waterford, and then along Ireland's S coast. This is a low-stress way of reaching the far SW, but it does take rather longer. The other possibility is to make for the Isles of Scilly first, where you can gradually absorb the rather exposed atmosphere and become accustomed to the proximity of the Atlantic. Having fuelled at Hugh Town, on St Mary's, you can reckon about 165 miles to Crookhaven—11 hours at 15 knots, 8¼ hours at 20 knots, and just over 6½ hours at 25 knots.

Fuel consumption is a vital factor, though, and you must have a generous reserve against the risk of adverse weather enforcing a slower speed than planned for the same engine revs. You can save a bit of distance by crossing to Kinsale, but that is perhaps best kept in hand as an alternative destination in case the wind freshens from the W while you are on passage.

Offshore fishing nets provide a significant hazard as you approach Fastnet, so keep your eyes peeled for lines of small floats or distant flags. The Cornish and Irish coasts show up well on radar, but you should make a landfall on the low-lying Scillies with caution. Off the Cornish coast there are Racon beacons on Wolf Rock lighthouse and the Seven Stones light-vessel. On the Irish side, Mizen Head has a Racon.

Newlyn is a handy port-of-call if you miss the tide for the Lizard or if, having made a late afternoon or evening landfall, you prefer not to tussle in the dark with that headland's race or numerous off-lying crab-pots. Although Newlyn harbour is busy with fishing boats, a visiting yacht can usually find a temporary overnight berth alongside the North Pier. Unlike Penzance, Newlyn is accessible at all states of tide. In moderate westerly weather there is a sheltered outside anchorage in Gwavas Lake, a couple of cables N of the pierheads.

Pilot Books, etc.

Admiralty NP27, *The Channel Pilot.*

Admiralty NP37, *West Coast of England and Wales Pilot.*

Admiralty NP40, *Irish Coast Pilot.*

Admiralty NP74, *List of Lights, Vol. A.*

Irish Cruising Club Sailing Directions, *South and West Coasts of Ireland* (recommended), available by post from Clyde Cruising Club Publications, S.V. 'Carrick', Clyde Street, Glasgow G1 4LN, Tel. 041 552 2183.

The Cruising Association Handbook, 7th edn 1990, published by the Cruising Association.

Charts

Admiralty:

No. 1123—Western Approaches to St George's Channel and Bristol Channel

No. 154—Approaches to Falmouth

No. 2565—St Agnes Head to Dodman Point, including the Isles of Scilly

No. 777—Land's End to Falmouth

No. 2345—Plans in South West Cornwall

No. 1148—Isles of Scilly to Land's End

No. 34—Isles of Scilly, including St Mary's Road

No. 2424—Kenmare River to Cork Harbour

No. 2184—Mizen Head to Gascanane Sound

No. 2129—Long Island Bay to Castlehaven

No. 2092—Toe Head to Old Head of Kinsale

No. 1765—Old Head of Kinsale to Power Head

No. 1777—Port of Cork, lower harbour and approaches

Imray:

C7—Lizard Point to Trevose Head and Scillies

C56—South West Coast of Ireland

Y57—Helford River to Falmouth Approaches

Y58—Falmouth Harbour and River Fal

Tidal Atlases

Stanford's Tidal Atlas, English Channel West (recommended).

Admiralty NP250, *English and Bristol Channels.*

Admiralty NP256, *Irish Sea.*

Tidal Streams (times based on HW Dover)

Position	E-going stream starts	W-going stream starts
3 miles S of the Lizard	+0330	−0145
5 miles N of Seven Stones light-vessel	+0610	−0045
5 miles SE of Fastnet Rock	+0300	−0330

	N-going stream starts	S-going stream starts
2 miles W of Longships	+0100	−0500
5 miles N of Seven Stones light-vessel	+0200	−0450

Tidal Differences and Heights

Place	Time of HW on Dover	Heights above chart datum in metres			
		MHWS	MLWS	MHWN	MLWN
Falmouth	−0605	5.3	0.6	4.2	1.9
Newlyn	+0600	5.6	0.8	4.4	2.0
Isles of Scilly (St Mary's)	+0600	5.7	0.7	4.3	2.0
Crookhaven	+0605	3.3	0.4	2.7	0.9
Kinsale	−0600	4.0	0.5	3.2	1.4
Cork harbour (near entrance)	−0550	4.0	0.5	3.2	1.3

Important Lights

English coast:

St Anthony Head, Falmouth (*Oc15s, WR, 22M, 20M, red sector shines over The Manacles 004°–022°T*); Lizard Point (*Fl3s, 29M*); Newlyn South Pier (*Fl5s, 9M, vis 253°–336°T*); Tater-Du (*Fl3, 15s, 23M, vis 241°– 074°T, and FR shines over Runnelstone, 14M, vis 060°– 074°T*); Runnelstone E-cardinal buoy (*Q6+LFl, 15s, bell, whistle*); Wolf Rock (*A1.FlWR, 30s, 23M, 22M*) **but note the following Notice to Mariners:** For about 9 months from 11 May 1987, the normal aids exhibited from the lighthouse will be discontinued. The tower will be marked by synchronized lights on each side showing (*Fl2, 10s, 32m, 5M*). In addition, the LANBY Wolf Rock (*Fl, 15s 24M*) will be temporarily established in *49°55'.40N, 05°48'.85W*. Longships (*IsoWR, 10s, 19M, 18M, 15M*); Pendeen (*Fl4, 15s, 27M*); Seven Stones light-vessel (*Fl3, 30s, 25M*); Round Island (*FlR, 10s, 24M, vis 021°– 288°T*); Bishop Rock (*Fl2, 15s, 29M*).

Irish coast:

Fastnet Rock (*Fl5s, 28M*); Mizen Head (*Iso4s, 16M, vis 313°–133°T*); Crookhaven, Rock Island Point (*LFlWR, 8s, 13M, 11M*); Galley Head (*Fl5, 20s, 28M, vis 256°– 065°T*); Old Head of Kinsale (*Fl2, 10s, 25M*); Kinsale Head Gas Field—West Well (*Mo(U)W, 15s, 15M and Mo(U)R, 15s, 3M*); East Well, as for West Well. Entrance to Cork Harbour, Roche's Point (*OcWR, 20s, 20M, 16M*); Cork Harbour (White Bay) leading lights in line 354°T (*synchronized, OcR, 5s, 5M*); Ballycotton Island (*FlWR, 10s, 22M, 18M*).

RDF Beacons

English coast:

Lizard Point (*298.8kHz, 'LZ', 70M, No. 6*); Land's End aero beacon (*114.2kHz, 'LND', cont.*); Penzance Heliport aero beacon (*333kHz, 'PH', 15M, 0800-2030*); Isles of Scilly, Round Island (*308kHz, 'RR', 100M, No. 5*); Isles of Scilly, St Mary's aero beacon (*321kHz, 'STM', 15M, cont.*)

Irish coast:

Mizen Head (*308kHz, 'MZ', 100M, no. 4*); Old Head of Kinsale (*296.5kHz, 'OH', 50M, No. 2*); Ballycotton Island (*296.5kHz, 'BN', 50M, No. 1*).

Weather Forecasts (all times GMT except where otherwise stated)

BBC shipping forecast areas:

Plymouth, Sole, Fastnet, Lundy

VHF coast radio stations:

Pendennis—0803, 2003, on Ch. 62

Land's End—0803, 2003, on Ch. 27 or 2670 kHz

Marinecall:

Tel. 0898 500 458 (can be useful for the first part of the passage of the Cornish coast)

Local radio coastal forecasts:

BBC Radio Cornwall—Mon–Fri at Local times 0628, 0715, 0745, 0815, 1245, 1645; Sat at 0745, 0815, 0843, 0915, 0945; Sun at 0915, 0943, 1015, 1045. Frequencies: *630/657 kHz, 476/457m, 95.2/96.0/ 103.9 MHz FM*

Met Office forecasts:

An overall view can be obtained from Plymouth Weather Centre, Tel. 0752 402534

13 MILFORD HAVEN TO ROSSLARE

The crossing of St George's Channel from Milford Haven to Rosslare is, at about 60 miles, one of the shorter passages covered in this book. It can, nevertheless, represent an important leg for S coast yachtsmen taking the 'coastal' route to Ireland. Although the Fastnet passage described in Chapter 12 is usually the quickest and most efficient way of reaching the magnificent cruising grounds of SW Ireland, this long open sea haul may not be everyone's choice. Lightly crewed yachts and motor boats with limited range will probably be better off making shorter hops when the weather serves.

In fact, you can reach Ireland in easy day passages if you have the time: Falmouth to Newlyn or Penzance perhaps (36 miles); Newlyn to St Ives (34 miles); St Ives to Padstow (32 miles); Padstow to Milford Haven (70 miles); Milford Haven to Rosslare, and thence along the Irish coast as the mood takes you.

The passage across St George's Channel is fairly straightforward, but you have to be careful with tides off the SW tip of Wales, until South Bishop lighthouse is safely astern. The streams run strongly around this corner of Pembrokeshire, especially between the various offshore islands and shoals. Skomer and Skokholm Islands are quite close to Milford Haven entrance, with Skokholm 3½ miles WNW of St Ann's Head and Skomer only 1½ miles N by W of Skokholm, just off Wooltack Point.

There are dangerous areas of overfalls immediately W of Skomer and Skokholm, most savage near springs when the streams can reach 4 or 5 knots locally. Grassholme, 6 miles W of Skomer, is more of an isolated skerry than an island. Bound for Rosslare, you'd normally pass between Grassholme and Skomer. The Smalls rocks lie 7 miles W by S of Grassholme, guarded by a lighthouse (*Fl3, 15s, 26M*). Two unmarked dangers lurk between the Smalls and Grassholme—the Hats, with only 2.1 m over them in parts, and the Barrels, which dry 3 m. Surrounded by overfalls and powerful tides, both these shoals should be avoided like the plague.

Milford Haven is a fine natural harbour and a very agreeable place from which to start a passage. Camper and Nicholson's attractive marina at Neyland is a useful base for laying in stores, fuel or water, although it is 7 miles upstream from the Haven entrance, on the N shore just below the Cleddau suspension bridge. When you are ready to leave the comforts of pontoon life, it is a good idea

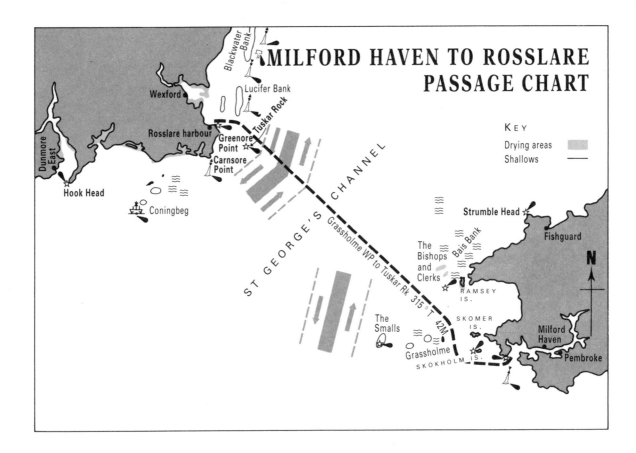

to drop down to the anchorage at Dale, whence you can easily slip out to sea when the tide and weather serve.

Other things being equal, the best time to leave Dale is about 3 hours before HW Milford Haven. The estuary flood will be weakly foul until you get out to St Ann's Head, but the main stream outside will be falling slack for half-an-hour or so before it begins to trickle W and N.

It is prudent to pass 1 mile S of Skokholm Island, making good a little S of W for a generous 6 miles from St Ann's Head to be sure of avoiding Wild Goose Race. Keep an eye on your position as you draw W of Skokholm Head, to guard against the early stream setting you N too soon. Once you are

well clear of Wild Goose Race, alter to the NNW so as to pass between Grassholme and Skomer, leaving Grassholme 2–2½ miles to the W.

The tide should now be running in your favour. A useful departure waypoint is Grassholme bearing SW, distant 2–3 miles. From here you can start sailing NW if the wind allows, a heading that will take you well clear of the South Bishop and set you on your way for Tuskar Rock, off the SE tip of Ireland. It is approximately 42 miles at 315°T from the Grassholme waypoint to a position 3 miles due N of the Tuskar. An ideal wind for this passage is probably a moderate easterly or north-easterly, although a south-westerly gives a comfortable reach so long as it is not too fresh. A fair-weather

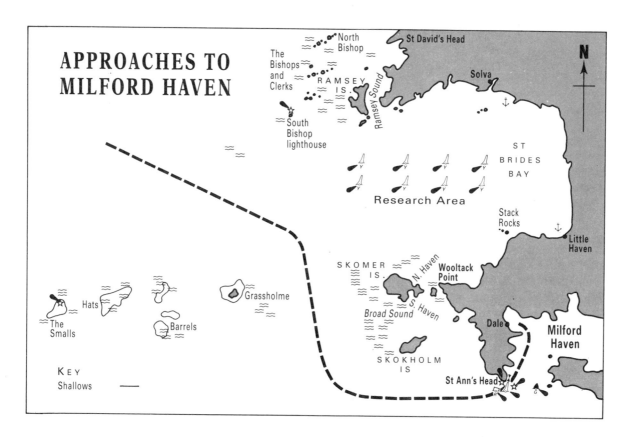

APPROACHES TO MILFORD HAVEN

north-westerly is, unfortunately, a dead noser.

The tides in St George's Channel set more or less NNE before and SSW after HW Dover. Maximum rates are around 3 knots at top springs, but between springs and neaps you will only be getting up to about 2 knots during the middle hours of the tide, with a mean rate of no more than 1.3 knots over a 6-hour period.

If you had left Dale 3 hours before HW Milford Haven (which is 4½ hours after HW Dover) and cleared Grassholme 2½–3 hours later, you would be setting off across the Channel with roughly 4 hours of NNE stream to run, a short spell of slack, and then 6 hours of SSW-going ebb. If you average 5 knots, your 42 miles should take just over 8 hours

and the tides will tend to cancel each other out. With an average of 4 knots, you would experience a net set to the SSW. Much depends upon the wind direction on the day.

The track to Rosslare crosses two sets of traffic separation schemes—one to the W of the Smalls and one close SE of Tuskar Rock. If, on your chart, you extend the Smalls lanes to the N, you will see that you can expect to meet shipping for a large part of the passage, once you have left the South Bishop 10 miles astern. Watch out for the Pembroke Dock to Rosslare ferries which will be following more or less the same line as you.

The landfall on the Irish coast is not difficult, even though it can seem bleak if the skies are grey and the wind a shade too fresh. Tuskar Rock stands alone 5 miles offshore, an imposing landmark on this SE corner of County Wexford, which is otherwise rather low and featureless. The final approaches to Rosslare harbour are shallow and a buoyed channel leads right to the outer pierhead from the ESE, but you should swing a bit wide when coming into the harbour in case a ferry is on her way out. Yachts on passage can usually find a sheltered berth on the W side of the *inner* pier, either at anchor or alongside a fishing boat.

Rosslare is a busy ferry port and has an active fishing co-operative. The pilot books often given the impression that Rosslare is distinctly austere, not the kind of place you would choose to go into except in an emergency. It is true that the sprawl of the ferry terminal is not exactly picturesque, yet I have always found the harbour itself rather snug, except in fresh north-westerlies. There are no local yachts, but the fishermen are a friendly crowd and it is only about 10–15 minutes' walk through the terminal concourse and up the hill to the shops and pubs. Rosslare is particularly well placed as a staging-post if you are planning to cruise farther up the E coast of Ireland.

Poor Visibility

The Welsh end of this passage is the trickiest in bad visibility, because of the need to avoid Wild Goose Race and steer well clear of the dangers that lie between Grassholme and the Smalls. It is not easy to estimate the tidal streams in this area and you need to be able to take frequent bearings to con yourself through.

Without a reliable Decca, the only feasible route in very murky conditions is to pass well S of the Smalls, preferably when the tide is slackish or S-going but allowing generously for the stream if it is

setting N. There is, alas, no useful RDF beacon to guide you out on this line, although the South Bishop beacon (*296.5, 'SB', 50M, No. 5*) will help you decide when you are safely W of the Smalls.

Shipping in St George's Channel can be a worry in poor visibility, although the traffic is nothing like as dense as in parts of the English Channel. The South Bishop and Tuskar Rock beacons are both useful on passage; their bearings can't be crossed to give an accurate position, but they will indicate whether or not you are on track between the two.

On the Irish side, a landfall in poor visibility requires a certain amount of ingenuity and is somewhat taxing on the nerves. Tuskar Rock beacon is reassuring (*296.5, 'TR', 50M, No. 6*), but the bad news is that to reach the Tuskar you have to negotiate the traffic separation scheme with an increasing risk of meeting ferries leaving or converging on Rosslare. Although Tuskar Rock is fairly steep-to, it still needs a reasonably wide berth as the tides tend to set towards it as you get near. It is also important not to come too close to the drying ledges off Greenore Point, the low promontory 1 mile or so SE of Rosslare pierhead.

The best plan is usually to navigate for Rosslare outer channel buoys as planned, not homing on to Tuskar Rock beacon but simply using its changing bearing to help confirm your estimated position. The tricky bit is deciding when to alter to the W towards Rosslare if you have not sighted any of the buoys by the time you have run your distance. So long as the sea is relatively calm, it is preferable to alter later rather than sooner—better to over-run on your original course and stray across the inshore banks than to turn W too soon and risk making a landfall near Greenore Point.

The echo-sounder can be informative over the shoals in the approaches to Rosslare. In calm or westerly weather, it may be wise to give up the idea of finding Rosslare pierhead in favour of edging into the bay somewhere between Rosslare harbour and Wexford and anchoring in shallow water until visibility improves.

Heavy Weather on Passage

Milford Haven to Rosslare is not a good heavy-weather passage, partly because of the strong tidal streams and various dangers off the SW tip of Wales, but also because your choice of alternative destinations is very limited. St George's Channel is not a pleasant stretch of water in heavy weather, especially when wind and tide are opposed, and it can serve up a particularly evil concoction of steep confused seas.

It is sound policy, therefore, to stay tucked up in Milford Haven if the forecast looks at all fringe. There is not even much scope for poking your nose out and 'giving it a try', because the tides may dictate that, once you are round the corner past Skokholm and Skomer, you are out there for some time. There are no secure harbours on the Pembroke peninsula between Milford Haven and Fishguard, which lies nearly 25 miles NE from South Bishop lighthouse, along a hostile stretch of coast complicated by the Bishops and Clerks rocks and the extensive race in the vicinity of Bais Bank.

However, it is worth bearing in mind one or two smaller bolt-holes not far from Milford Haven, which can be useful in certain conditions if you have put to sea and rather wish that you hadn't. Skomer has two natural anchorages, North Haven being snug in winds with any S in them and South Haven offering good shelter from W through N to E. The problem with these anchorages is that tide and sea conditions locally can make them tricky to reach. The best approach to South Haven from Milford Haven is by passing E of Skokholm, but

that is not the route you'd normally take when setting off for Rosslare. To approach South Haven from seaward means negotiating the races W of Skokholm and Skomer. North Haven is better placed in this respect, providing the wind is in a safe quarter, because you can decide to turn back for North Haven once you have passed between Grassholme and Skomer.

You might consider North Haven if you have set off from Dale in a wind from between SE and SW which turns out to be stronger than expected. A south-easterly, for example, will mean a hard slog back to Milford Haven if the NW-going stream has gathered momentum, whereas it may not be so painful to slip round Skomer into North Haven. The final approach to North Haven is from due N, keeping to the W side of the entrance to avoid the drying reef which extends NNW from The Neck. The passage E of Skomer through Jack Sound should only be taken in quiet weather, preferably at slack water but certainly not when the tide is foul.

South Haven can serve a similar purpose in north-westerlies or north-easterlies, although it will probably be easier to run back to Milford Haven S of Skokholm than to negotiate Broad Sound and its races. To enter South Haven, first make for the Mewstone, right at the S tip of Skomer, and then keep well over to the W side of the inlet as you go in.

The sweep of St Brides Bay opens up to the NE of Skomer. The streams are weak in the bay and the coast clean, although the protection it can offer is very limited. In winds from between S and E, there is a good anchorage in the SE corner of St Brides, close inshore between Borough Head and Little Haven. In winds from between N and E, there is a sheltered cove on the N side of the bay, between Solva Creek and a promontory known as Dinas-fawr.

Solva Creek itself is shallow and the entrance

narrow, but there is shelter inside for boats that can edge upstream a little way and take the ground. It would make a feasible bolt-hole if, having passed between Grassholme and Skomer early on the N-going tide, you met a north-westerly which was stronger than anticipated but you were wary about running back to Milford Haven against the increasingly powerful weather-going stream. Enter Solva within 2 hours of local HW, keeping over to the E to leave the westernmost islet in the entrance (Black Rock) close to port.

Fishguard harbour, just over 3 miles E of Strumble Head, would probably only come to mind as a possible refuge if you were well on your way across the Channel and met freshening winds from the W or NW. Fishguard is accessible in any weather, by day or night, whatever the tide. Strumble Head (*Fl4, 15s, 29M*) is a prominent headland on which to make a landfall, but the offshore streams are strong about 1 mile N of Strumble. Bais Bank, the shallowest part (7.8 m) of which lies 11 miles WSW of Strumble Head, should be given a wide berth in heavy weather.

At the Irish end of this passage, there are few options for bolt-holes in the event of heavy weather. Given, for example, an earlier-than-expected Atlantic depression and a strengthening south-westerly or westerly, it is usually a case of shortening sail, gritting your teeth, and pressing on for Rosslare.

Wexford Harbour lies a few miles N of Rosslare, but the shallow entrance has a bar which is dangerous in strong onshore winds. There is no other port of refuge on the E coast of Ireland until you get to Arklow, nearly 35 miles N of Rosslare, and this also has a dangerous entrance in onshore gales. Perhaps the only circumstances in which you might decide to make for Arklow would be if, half-way across St George's Channel, you met with a strong westerly which had some N in it. You wouldn't be able to lay the course for Rosslare, but it would be feasible to ease off towards Arklow, with the intention of working into the partial lee of the land somewhere safely N of the Blackwater Bank.

Heavy weather from the NW would be a decided nuisance on the passage from Milford Haven to Rosslare. Fishguard was suggested as a possibility if you had not reached the point of no return, but it would be a shame to run back to the Welsh coast if you were well over towards the Tuskar when things started to blow up. Rather than trying to claw up to windward for Rosslare, you might decide to stay on the starboard tack and make for Dunmore East, at the entrance to Waterford Harbour. Much would depend on how much N there was in the wind and whether you could manage to hold up towards the S coast in order to obtain some lee from the land. Waterford entrance is about 23 miles W of Carnsore Point—quite a long diversion, but one that might look attractive if the wind was more N than NW, up to Force 6 or 7 and rising.

The Return Passage

The main factor to keep in mind about the return passage is the need to time the tides for the last leg between South Bishop and St Ann's Head. A useful landfall waypoint is a position 5 miles or so due W of South Bishop lighthouse, from where you can reckon about 20 miles to Milford Haven entrance. Other things being equal, a good time to arrive at this waypoint is at HW Dover or soon afterwards, to catch the start of the SE-going stream which will carry you down between Grassholme and Skomer and then round to the W and S of Skokholm.

Making a landfall on this SW corner of Wales, it is almost always preferable to be well up to the N near the South Bishop waypoint, where you can fix your position and plot a safe course down between the islands. If you make a landfall further S, you risk being set too close to the dangers between the Smalls and Grassholme. This strategy holds good to an even greater extent in poor visibility. So long as the tide is flowing S as you approach the South Bishop, you can come within ½ mile of the light-house if necessary, homing on to its RDF beacon

and listening for the fog signal (*3 horn blasts ev 45s*). In very murky weather, so long as the wind is not fresh from the W, the safest course from there is to make for an anchorage at the head of St Brides Bay, where the streams are weak, the coast is clear of dangers, and the gradually shelving depths give you fair warning of your position.

High-speed Factors

The 60-mile crossing from Milford Haven to Rosslare is a convenient route to Ireland for anyone planning to cruise the E coast. In quiet weather, at 15–20 knots, you can plan for a pleasant morn-ing or afternoon run, but it must be admitted that St George's Channel is not renowned for long spells of calm. It is an uneasy stretch of water, especially on the Welsh side where the strong streams and overfalls can soon create malevolent conditions in a fresh wind.

Navigators of fast motor boats should always try to time their departure from or arrival off the SW tip of Wales for slack water, which is either 5–6 hours after or 2–2½ hours before HW Milford Haven. The various tidal races in the vicinity of Skomer, Skokholm and Grassholme will then be resting for a while and you can hope to slip past unmolested.

The passage waypoints used in the main part of this chapter are equally suitable for motor boats, and both sides of the crossing provide reasonable radar

targets. On the Irish side, Tuskar Rock shows up well and the lighthouse has an 18-mile Racon beacon. As you approach the Tuskar, you can begin to identify the coast between Carnsore Point and Greenore Point. On the Welsh side, St David's Head and Ramsey Island are prominent as you come in from the NW, although South Bishop lighthouse doesn't always show clearly until you get quite close. The Smalls lighthouse has a 25-mile Racon beacon.

Pilot Books, etc.

Admiralty NP37, *West Coast of England and Wales Pilot.*

Admiralty NP40, *Irish Coast Pilot.*

Admiralty NP74, *List of Lights, Vol. A.*

The Cruising Association Handbook, 7th edn 1990, published by the Cruising Association.

Bristol Channel and Severn Pilot, P. Cumberlidge, 1988, published by Stanford Maritime.

Lundy, Fastnet and Irish Sea Pilot, vol. I. *The Bristol Channel*, D. Taylor, 1988, published by Imray Laurie Norie and Wilson.

Irish Cruising Club Sailing Directions, vols I and II, available by post from Clyde Cruising Club Publications, S.V. 'Carrick', Clyde Street, Glasgow G1 4LN, Tel. 041 552 2138.

Admiralty Charts

No. 2878—Approaches to Milford Haven

No. 1478—St Govan's Head to St David's Head

No. 1482—Plans on the south and west coasts of Dyfed

No. 1410—St George's Channel

No. 1973—Cardigan Bay—southern part

No. 1787—Carnsore Point to Wicklow Head

No. 1772—Rosslare and Wexford harbours with approaches

Tidal Atlases

Admiralty NP250, *English and Bristol Channels.*

Admiralty NP256, *Irish Sea.*

Tidal Streams (times based on HW Dover)

Position	N-going stream starts	S-going stream starts
Between Skomer and Grassholme	+0545	HW
5 miles W of South Bishop lighthouse	+0550	−0030
4 miles E of Tuskar Rock	+0550	−0030

Tidal Differences and Heights

Place	Time of HW on Dover	Heights above chart datum in metres			
		MHWS	MLWS	MHWN	MLWN
Dale	−0500	7.0	0.7	5.2	2.5
Skomer	−0455	6.6	0.7	5.1	2.5
Little Haven	−0450	5.9	0.7	4.4	2.3
Solva Creek	−0450	5.5	0.7	4.2	2.3
Fishguard	−0355	4.8	0.8	3.5	2.1
Rosslare	−0510	2.0	0.4	1.5	0.9
Wexford	−0305 (Sp)	1.7	0.2	1.4	0.5
	−0625 (Np)				
Arklow	−0150	1.1	–	1.0	–
Dunmore East	−0530	4.5	0.4	3.6	1.2

Important Lights

Pembrokeshire coast:

St Ann's Head (*FIWR, 5s, W23M, R22M, R19M; W 230°-247°T, R 247°-285°T, R(intens) 285°-314°T, R 314°-332°T, W 332°-124°T, W 129°-131°T*); Middle Channel Rocks (*Fl3G, 7s, 8M*); Skokholm Head (*FlR, 10s, 17M, partially obscured 226°-258°T*); The Smalls (*Fl3, 15s, 25M; FR, 13M, vis 253°-285°T over Hats and Barrels*); South Bishop (*Fl, 5s, 24M*); Strumble Head (*Fl4, 15s, 29M*).

Irish coast:

Tuskar Rock (*Q2, 7½s, 28M*); Rosslare main pierhead (*WRG, 5s, 13M, 10M, 10M; G 098°-188°T, W 188°-208°T, R 208°-246°T, G 246°-283°T, W 283°-286°T, R 286°-320°T*); Rosslare inner pierhead (*Q, 3M*); Coningbeg light float (*Fl3, 30s, 24M*); Hook Head, E side of Waterford harbour entrance (*Fl, 3s, 24M*); Dunmore East E pierhead (*FIWR, 8s, 12M, 9M; W 225°-310°T, R 310°-004°T*); Arklow LANBY (*Fl2, 12s, 16M*); Arklow S pierhead (*FIWR, 6s, 13M; R shore-223°T, W 223°-350°T, 350°-shore*); Arklow N pierhead (*LFIG, 7s, 10M; vis shore-287°T*).

RDF Beacons

South Bishop lighthouse (*296.5kHz, 'SB', 50M, No. 5*); Tuskar Rock lighthouse (*296.5kHz, 'TR', 50M, no. 6*).

Weather Forecasts (all times GMT except where otherwise stated)

BBC shipping forecast areas:

    Lundy, Fastnet, Irish Sea

VHF coast radio stations:

    Celtic Radio—0803, 2003, on Ch. 24

Met Office forecasts:

    Useful overall view can be obtained from Cardiff Weather Centre, Tel. 0222 397020

14 ISLE OF MAN CROSSINGS

Beset by a rather forbidding reputation, the Irish Sea is at least a fairly compact stretch of water, made more so by the Isle of Man's strategic potential as a staging-post. On the English side, the coasts of Cumbria and Lancashire are unfamiliar to most cruising yachtsmen, sailing activity having been largely confined to local pockets of enthusiasts who have made the most of the few havens to be found there. The situation is changing a little now, with the development of Liverpool Marina on the Mersey and, more recently, Maryport Marina up on the S shore of the Solway Firth.

The N coast of Wales is perhaps even less hospitable, until you get along to the attractive Menai Strait. Things are generally more friendly over on the Irish side, which offers an uncomplicated weather shore against the prevailing winds and has Carrickfergus Marina, Bangor, Strangford Lough and Carlingford Lough all within a day's sail of the Isle of Man.

The Isle of Man has an interesting selection of harbours and anchorages, although there is nowhere to lie afloat which is completely protected from all quarters. Douglas outer harbour is secure except in strong easterlies or north-easterlies, but has limited room for visiting yachts. Ramsey Bay, 7 miles N of Douglas, is good in westerlies but open to the E. At the S tip of the island, Port St Mary is snug in winds from between N and W, and Castletown is sheltered in north-easterlies.

On the W coast, Peel is protected from between E through S to SW and Port Erin is a safe bet in winds with any E in them. One drawback of the Isle of Man is that all the W coast havens are open to the W, all the E coast havens are open to the E, and it can be a long haul from one side of the island to the other if the wind shifts unexpectedly.

There are possible crossings to the Isle of Man from all points of the compass. Up on the Cumbrian coast you have four closely spaced harbours at Whitehaven, Harrington, Workington and Maryport. Whitehaven dries, but offers good shelter at the inner quays and can be entered in heavy weather if the tide serves. Harrington is a small drying pier harbour, not quite 4 miles N of Whitehaven, which is used and run by the friendly Harrington Sailing and Fishing Club. Workington, 2½ miles farther N, is accessible at almost any state of tide and you can stay afloat in the turning basin so long as you keep clear of ships manoeuvring. Maryport, 5 miles N of Workington, has been closed for many years but now has a new marina which can be

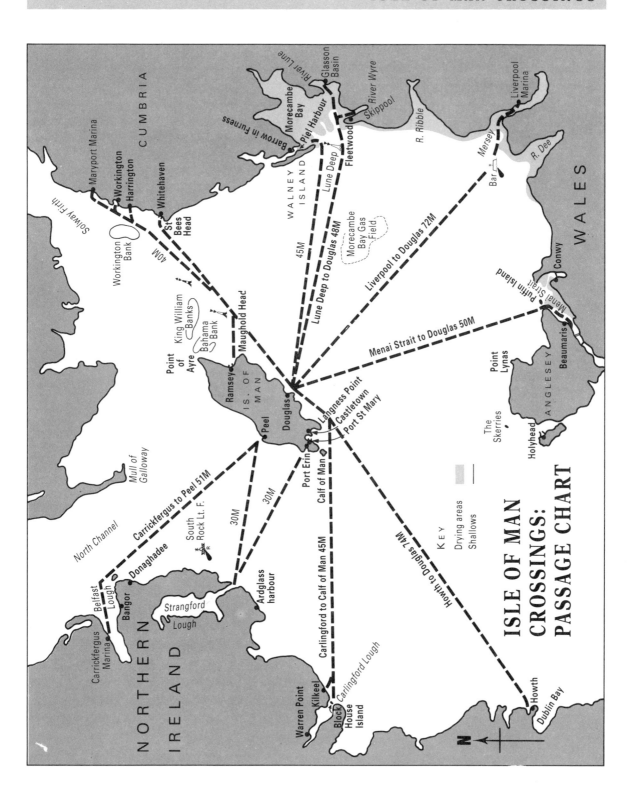

entered via a lock 4 hours or so either side of HW.

Further S on the Lancashire coast, Morecambe Bay offers one or two havens, of which Glasson Basin is the most agreeable and secure for yachts. Six miles up the River Lune from Fleetwood fairway buoy, this well-appointed marina within Glasson Dock is accessible via a lock for 1½ hours before HW. Fleetwood is a busy port, but you can leave or enter at any state of tide and anchor in the River Wyre a little way S of the entrance to the docks.

There are a number of drying pile moorings at Skippool Creek, some 5 miles up the Wyre above Fleetwood. Blackpool and Fleetwood Yacht Club have their base here and they give a warm welcome to any visitor who finds his way up. There are also some moorings a little way below Skippool at Hambleton. Over on the N side of Morecambe Bay, there is shelter behind Walney Island in Piel harbour and the Walney Channel. Although Piel bar has 2 m at LAT, strangers should enter or leave above half-tide. The Walney Channel leads up to Barrow in Furness, 3 miles from the entrance.

The Ribble Estuary lies 12 miles S of Morecambe Bay, but it is a long haul up a shallow channel past wide sandflats to the drying moorings at Lytham or Freckleton. It is safest not to rely on any shelter between Fleetwood and the Mersey, where you can lock into Liverpool Marina on the N bank opposite Tranmere.

There are no useful havens along the N coast of Wales until you get as far W as Conwy and the entrance to the Menai Strait. Conwy harbour almost dries at LAT, although most boats will stay afloat at neaps. The final approach to Conwy is from the W and strangers should not proceed beyond the fairway buoy until half-flood. Between Anglesey and the mainland, the Menai Strait offers good shelter and some very picturesque anchor-ages. The entrance from the N leads between Puffin Island and Anglesey and thence SW along the buoyed channel to Beaumaris.

Crossing to the Isle of Man from Ireland, you have a good selection of harbours from which to leave. Up in Belfast Lough, Carrickfergus Marina and Bangor harbour are secure ports of call, accessible at any state of tide. A few miles S of the entrance to Belfast Lough, Donaghadee harbour is sheltered from the W and Copelands Marina is accessible a couple of hours either side of HW.

The narrow entrance to Strangford Lough lies 20 miles S of Donaghadee, just opposite the Isle of Man. There are numerous small islands and sheltered anchorages in this fascinating inlet, which is nearly 12 miles long and mostly about 2 miles wide. Ardglass harbour is 5 miles S round the coast from Strangford, well sheltered from the W but exposed to the SE. Kilkeel fishing harbour lies 18 miles SW of Ardglass, accessible above half-tide; this is very much a working port, but the occasional visiting yacht can be squeezed in right at the far end of the inner basin.

Carlingford Lough lies a few miles SW of Kilkeel, on the border between Northern Ireland and the Republic. The narrow entrance channel into Carlingford leads between the N shore and Block House Island, and it is difficult to leave or enter against the tide. Inside the Lough it is possible to find a sheltered anchorage in almost any wind, although in fresh north-westerlies you have to go up to Warren Point, 8 miles above the entrance.

Howth Marina, just N of Dublin Bay, is a full day's sail from the Isle of Man and about the same distance SW of Douglas as Liverpool Marina is to the SE. Since Howth is easy of access, well sheltered and has excellent facilities, it makes a good passage harbour for anyone cruising the W side of the Irish Sea.

None of the Isle of Man crossings from the harbours I have mentioned is particularly long—Howth or Liverpool to Douglas represent the longest legs at 75 miles, and Whitehaven to Ramsey Bay is only 30 miles. The difficulty with most of the passages is that, if you are overtaken by heavy weather, alternative ports of refuge may be few and far between. The geography of this area also means that there is usually a lee shore not too far away, wherever a blow might be coming from. If conditions are at all uncertain, therefore, it is important to plan your passage so that you have some kind of alternative strategy to fall back on.

North Cumbria Coast to the Isle of Man

You can reckon just under 40 miles from Maryport Marina to Ramsey harbour, at the NE end of the Isle of Man. From Whitehaven to Ramsey is more like 30 miles and from Workington or Harrington about 35 miles. The passages are similar except that Maryport is situated on the outer navigable reaches of the Solway Firth; leaving from here means that you have 8 miles of relatively shoal water to negotiate before clearing Workington Bank and reaching open sea.

Coming from Maryport or Workington, your departure waypoint will probably be near Workington Bank S-cardinal buoy, which lies 3 miles SW of Workington pierhead. From this position, 24 miles at 225°T takes you across to Bahama Bank S-cardinal buoy, moored at the SE tip of a narrow shoal extending 8 miles or so from the Point of Ayre. This track leaves King William Banks E-cardinal buoy not quite 1 mile to the W. Ramsey lies 8 miles W by S from the Bahama buoy, leaving Maughold Head 1½ miles to the S. Coming from Harrington or Whitehaven, your first leg will be straight to the Bahama buoy—about 26 miles at 229°T or 23 miles at 235°T respectively.

The tides for these crossings can be quite strong at springs, up to 3½ knots in the area immediately E of the banks. A good time to leave Maryport is 1 hour or so before HW Dover, say 1¾ hours before local HW. The last of the flood will still be setting into the Solway Firth, but it won't be long before the stream falls slack and then starts running broadly WSW.

The ebb and early flood will be more or less fair for the next 8 hours, before you pick up an increasing ESE-going stream 5 hours before the next HW Dover. This set is strongest near the King William Banks, so it is best to have averaged at least 4 knots and reached the Bahama buoy by this time. At this speed, you should arrive at Ramsey at half-flood, about 1 hour early for entering the inner harbour but no problem for the anchorage.

Coming from Workington, Harrington or Whitehaven, and given the same sort of average speed, you can leave a bit later, say ½ hour before local HW, and carry a fair tide for most of your passage.

Poor Visibility

None of these passages is difficult in poor visibility if conditions are fairly quiet, although the navigator will have an easier job near neaps. Coming from Maryport, you have to find your way down to Workington Bank S-cardinal buoy, but the soundings are helpful hereabouts and, by leaving 1 hour before HW Dover, the tidal offset will be slight for the first couple of hours. There is no problem about straying over Workington Bank in calm weather—you can, in fact, sound your way down the E side of the shoal water until you pick up the buoy (which has a bell).

As you approach King William Banks, the tide

should be setting away from the shoals rather than towards them. In very murky weather, the soundings give a better clue to your progress if you pass just *inside* the Bahama buoy (which also has a bell). Bearings from Point of Ayre and Douglas RDF beacons cut well in this area. The last leg to Ramsey is straightforward, with the streams weak and the coast clear of dangers. It is preferable to err on the side of making a landfall N of Ramsey rather than to the S; even if you can't find the harbour, it will then be safe to continue W until you run inside the 5 m line and can anchor.

Heavy Weather on Passage

The good news about the crossings from the North Cumbria coast to the Isle of Man is that they are comparatively short and you'd be very unlucky to be caught out without warning. The Isle of Man also provides a certain amount of lee in southwesterlies, even if you are only halfway to Ramsey or Douglas. The bad news is that neither Maryport, Workington or Whitehaven are particularly easy ports of refuge if you have to run back in a rising wind. Harrington is not suitable for strangers to approach in heavy weather.

The approaches to Maryport are shallow and the sea breaks heavily in strong onshore winds. There is also a bar near the S pier with only 1.8 m over it at half-flood, so you would only want to enter near HW in adverse conditions. In heavy weather from between S and W, especially if visibility is poor, you also have the problem of finding the Workington Bank S-cardinal buoy and leaving it to port so as to enter the English Channel.

Workington also has a bar, which extends for just over ¼ mile N of the coastguard station at the end of the S pier. In heavy onshore weather you'd only attempt to enter within about 2 hours of HW. The final approach is from the NW, bringing the leading lights into line bearing 131°T. Whitehaven has the simplest entrance and approach of the three, being a straightforward pier harbour, but you still wouldn't want to try and get in below half-tide in strong onshore winds.

In heavy south-easterly weather it would normally be safe to fetch back to Whitehaven, Workington or Maryport, provided you could keep close under St Bees Head and obtain increasing shelter from the coast. If, on the other hand, you were caught by a stiff north-westerly, there wouldn't be much choice but to shorten sail and press on until the Isle of Man provided some lee.

A strong north-easterly or easterly can be tricky, because you may not be able to gauge its weight until you are well on your way. If you are caught by winds from this direction which turn out to be stronger than expected, there is much to be said for making for Douglas rather than Ramsey. Although Douglas outer harbour is uncomfortable in strong winds from the E, at least it is safe and easy to enter at any state of tide. Heading for Douglas also gives you the option of running past the SE coast of the island to seek shelter in Castletown or Port St Mary.

Morecambe Bay to the Isle of Man

Morecambe Bay harbours three bases for yachtsmen: Piel and the Walney Channel on the N side; Fleetwood and Skippool Creek on the S side; and Glasson Basin Yacht Harbour, an attractive and well sheltered dock marina on the S bank of the River Lune, 6 miles upstream from Lune Channel No. 1 fairway buoy. Douglas is the nearest Isle of Man harbour to any of these three, although it is only an hour or two farther to reach Castletown or Port St Mary.

Coming from Glasson Basin, Fleetwood or Skippool, your departure waypoint would be somewhere between Danger Patch red can buoy and Lune Deep S-cardinal buoy, depending on the sea conditions and tide. Boats from Glasson have to lock out during the hour before local HW, which means a departure from the mouth something like 2–2½ hours after HW Dover. By this time you have lost a couple of hours of slack or favourable stream, but the only way to avoid this is to wait a complete tide at Fleetwood and then leave there 1½–2 hours before the next local HW.

Coming from Piel, your departure would be from the N side of the Morecambe estuary, somewhere between Lightning Knoll red-and-white fairway buoy and Halfway red can buoy. If you leave Piel 1½–2 hours before local HW and stem the last of the flood, you will pick up the best of the favourable stream out in the offing.

The passage from the Lune Deep buoy to Douglas is about 48 miles at 286°T, and from Lightning Knoll you can reckon on 45 miles at 281°T. These tracks lead 7–10 miles N of the Morecambe Bay Gas Field, an area which needs to be given a wide berth, with its various well-head buoys and gas platforms. A moderate north-easterly is a good wind for the passage, giving you a broad reach and a certain amount of lee from the Cumbrian coast. Fresh winds from the W are not good news, because they kick up steep seas in the approaches to Morecambe Bay.

Poor Visibility

Leaving Morecambe Bay is not much fun in murky visibility, although it is feasible to pick your way carefully from buoy to buoy. Once you are out in open water there are no real problems, with Walney Island RDF beacon (*287.3kHz, 'FN', 30M, Nos. 1, 4*)

giving you a useful back-bearing and Douglas Victoria Pier beacon (*287.3kHz, 'DG', 50M, Nos. 3, 6*) taking you right up to the harbour entrance. Point of Ayre beacon (*301.1kHz, 'PY', 50M, No. 5*) can usefully be crossed with Douglas as you approach the Isle of Man.

Heavy Weather on Passage

If strong winds look likely, it is best not to set off unless you are prepared to stay at sea and take things as you find them. A freshening south-westerly can make it difficult to lay the course for Douglas, although you have the option of freeing off and making for Ramsey. Perhaps even more inconvenient is an early veer to NW as a cold front passes through, giving you a long beat to windward. In a very hard north-westerly you might turn back for Fleetwood, but careful navigation is important so that you arrive at Lune Deep buoy and stay in the main entrance channel. A strong easterly wind will make you reluctant to turn back for the weather shore you have just left. Douglas is safe to enter in strongish onshore winds, but in severe conditions it would be better to round the Calf of Man a couple of miles off and then tuck into Port Erin.

Liverpool Marina to the Isle of Man

This is a longish haul, about 72 miles in total from the marina lock to Douglas harbour entrance. Liverpool Marina is accessible for 2 hours either side of HW, but the most practical time to lock out is about 1 hour before HW. You will then push the last dregs of the flood, have ½ hour of slack water, and pick up the first couple of hours of ebb before it gets too powerful in the lower reaches of the river. Down in the Queens Channel, a wind over the strong tide can raise a nasty steep sea in the best traditions of wide, fast-flowing estuaries. Neaps are preferable for this reason, and a neap HW is early in the morning at Liverpool, which gives you a full day for passage-making.

It is important to stay in the well-buoyed channel, as there are training banks on both sides of the fairway. Watch out for large tankers anywhere in the Mersey and its approaches. Your departure waypoint will be within a mile or two of the Bar LANBY, the track for Douglas being something like 313°T. If you leave the marina 1 hour before local HW and average 4½–5 knots coming downstream, you should be taking your departure 2 hours after local HW, which is 2¼ hours after HW Dover. You will then have 4 hours of stream setting you W by N, and then 6 hours setting more or less E. The middle period of the new flood can be quite strong, up to 2½ knots at springs.

Poor Visibility

The Mersey estuary is no joke in poor visibility, with ships and fast tides to contend with. Things are more straightforward once you are on passage, although it is important to stay well to the W of Morecambe Bay Gas Field. Approaching Douglas is no problem in mist or fog, by homing on to Victoria Pier RDF beacon.

Heavy Weather on Passage

Most yachts would not set off from the Mersey in fresh winds from the W, because of the grim conditions in the lower estuary. You really need a good forecast for a passage to the Isle of Man, because your options are limited if heavy weather pounces on the way. Other than turning back or pressing on, Fleetwood is the only possibility if the wind freshens from between NW and SW, but you have to be able to pass well clear of the gas field. In a strong north-easterly, it is safer to carry on or turn back than to run down towards the narrow entrance of the Menai Strait.

Menai Strait to the Isle of Man

In some respects, the 50-mile passage from the N end of the Menai Strait to the S tip of the Isle of Man is the most straightforward of this collection of crossings. Although not the shortest, it leads across an open stretch of water whose only complication is a certain amount of Liverpool shipping on its way round Anglesey. The direct track to Douglas is about 343°T.

The Menai Strait only just manages to separate Anglesey from NW Wales, yet it has a unique and strangely charged atmosphere. The narrowness of the channel creates scenic drama of course, as do the fast tides that scour at up to 6 knots through the Swellies. But despite the solidity of the bridges, you also sense that the Strait is a truly historic crossing point, a place where one of Robert Louis Stevenson's heros might have emerged from the undergrowth, summoned the ferryman to take him across the water, and sworn the poor chap to secrecy with the tip of his sword.

The attractive anchorage at Beaumaris overlooks the broad expanse of Lavan Sands and is only 4 miles from Puffin Island and the N entrance to the Strait. The favourable ebb starts running off Beaumaris 1½ hours after HW Dover. If you cast off at around this time and average 4½–5 knots, you should pick up a simple pattern of tides for the passage to the Isle of Man—5 hours of W-going stream, 1 hour of slack, and then 5 hours of E-going.

In poor visibility, there is a useful selection of RDF beacons: the Skerries and Point Lynas on

Anglesey; Cregneish and Douglas on the Isle of Man. There are generally few choices to be made if heavy weather catches you unawares: to press on, turn back if conditions allow, or stay at sea. The line of approach to the Isle of Man makes it relatively easy to opt for the E or W coasts, depending on the best prospects for shelter.

Crossings to and from Ireland

There are numerous permutations of crossings between Ireland and the Isle of Man. They tend to be easier passages than those from England or Wales, with moderate tides and more ports-of-call to choose from. The shortest is 30 miles, from Strangford Lough to Peel or Port Erin. Strangford is an interesting and convenient cruising ground to make for if you have come across to the Isle of Man from Cumbria, Lancashire or the Mersey and have some time to spare to see something of Northern Ireland. It is about 46 miles from Douglas to Strangford Lough fairway buoy, going S-about round the Calf of Man. The tides are strong between Langness Point and the Calf, the W-going stream starting ¼ hour after and the E-going stream 6 hours before HW Dover. Keep a good mile off Langness and Chicken Rock to avoid the races.

The entrance to Carlingford Lough lies about 45 miles W by S from the Calf of Man and makes a good day sail from Port St Mary or Castletown.

Kilkeel, just N of Carlingford, is worth bearing in mind if you miss the tide into the Lough. A rather longer passage separates the Isle of Man and Howth Yacht Club Marina, just N of Dublin Bay. You can reckon about 74 miles from Douglas to Howth, and you only save 7 miles by leaving from Port St Mary. Douglas to Carrickfergus Marina is a similar distance via the Calf of Man, but boats from Carrickfergus can reach Peel, on the E coast of the island, with a more modest haul of 51 miles.

Poor visibility between Ireland and the Isle of Man shouldn't provide a serious problem for most navigators. Although the Irish side is not well served with RDF beacons, there are various stretches of coast which are safe to approach in fog using soundings. The Isle of Man has a good selection of beacons.

Heavy weather is usually less of a headache between Ireland and the Isle of Man than it is on the English side, because the Irish coast provides a lee in gales from the W or SW, which are by far the most frequent. Strong easterlies or south-easterlies are not good news, though, since Carlingford Lough is not safe to approach in heavy onshore weather and Strangford Lough can only be entered on the flood in such conditions. If possible, you should make for the E side of the Isle of Man, where Peel and Port Erin are snug in winds from the E and SE.

High-speed Factors

In some respects, this area offers a better cruising ground for motor boats than it does for yachts, despite the Irish Sea's dubious reputation. The distances are relatively short, and it is usually a distinct advantage to be able to make quick passages between the Isle of Man and the mainland when sea conditions happen to be suitable.

The waypoints and routes described in the main part of this chapter are equally appropriate for power boats as for yachts, although passage times will be much shorter and the effects of the tidal streams will differ as a result. If possible, however, it is a good idea to try to schedule your departures so that you have a certain amount of 'abort time' available in which to get back to the harbour you have just left if sea conditions turn out to be more hostile than expected.

The Isle of Man provides a good radar target from all directions, although from some distance off you often pick up the mountains inland before the coast itself appears. Point of Ayre lighthouse has a useful Racon beacon ('M', 15M, 30s sweep). On the mainland there are Racons on Lune Deep S-cardinal buoy (10M), the Bar LANBY (10M), Skerries lighthouse (25M), Kish Bank lighthouse (15M) and South Rock light-vessel (13M).

Pilot Books, etc.

Admiralty NP37, *West Coast of England and Wales Pilot.*

Admiralty NP40, *Irish Coast Pilot.*

Admiralty NP74, *List of Lights, Vol. A.*

The Cruising Association Handbook, 7th edn 1990, published by the Cruising Association.

Irish Cruising Club Sailing Directions, *East and North Coasts of Ireland*, available by post from Clyde Cruising Club Publications, S.V. 'Carrick', Clyde Street, Glasgow G1 4LN, Tel. 041 552 2183.

Cruising Guide to the Isle of Man, R. Kemp, 1st edn 1979, published by Brown Son & Ferguson.

Cruising Guide to Anglesey and Menai Strait, R. Kemp, 1st edn 1979 (reprinted 1988), published by Brown Son & Ferguson.

Admiralty Charts

No. 1826—Irish Sea, Eastern Part

No. 1411—Irish Sea, Western Part

No. 2696—Harbours on the Isle of Man

No. 2013—Harbours on the Cumbrian coast

No. 2010—Morecambe Bay

No. 1978—Great Ormes Head to Liverpool

No. 1977—Holyhead to Great Ormes Head

No. 2800—Carlingford Lough and Kilkeel Harbour

No. 2156—Strangford Lough

No. 1753—Belfast Lough

Tidal Atlases

Admiralty NP256, *Irish Sea.*

Tidal Streams (times based on HW Dover)

Position	N/E-going stream starts	S/W-going stream starts
E of Workington Bank	−0445	+0115
Off Lune Deep buoy	−0500	+0045
5 miles E of Douglas harbour	−0515	+0015
Near the Bar LANBY	−0515	+0130
3 miles N of Puffin Island	−0545	+0015
Off Strangford Lough entrance	+0015	+0545

Tidal Differences and Heights

Place	Time of HW on Dover	Heights above chart datum in metres			
		MHWS	MLWS	MHWN	MLWN
Douglas	+0020	6.9	0.8	5.4	2.4
Port St Mary	+0025	5.9	0.6	4.7	1.7
Port Erin	+0020	5.2	0.4	4.2	1.6
Peel	+0015	5.3	0.5	4.2	1.5
Ramsey	+0020	7.3	0.8	5.8	2.4
Maryport	+0040	8.6	0.9	6.6	2.5
Workington	+0025	8.4	0.9	6.4	2.5
Whitehaven	+0015	8.2	0.9	6.3	2.6
Piel harbour	+0030	9.1	1.0	7.1	2.8
Glasson	+0050	9.5	1.1	7.4	3.1
Fleetwood	+0015	9.5	1.2	7.6	3.1
Liverpool	+0015	9.3	0.9	7.4	2.9
Conwy	−0030	7.6	0.7	5.9	2.3
Beaumaris	−0010	7.6	0.9	5.8	2.1
Carlingford	+0025	4.8	0.7	4.3	1.8
Kilkeel	+0015	5.3	0.7	4.4	1.9
Strangford	+0020	4.5	0.5	3.8	1.2

Important Lights

Isle of Man:
Point of Ayre (*Alt.LFl, WR, 60s, 19M; Low Lt Fl, 3s, 8M*);
Maughold Head (*Fl3, 30s, 22M*); Douglas Head (*Fl, 10s, 24M*); Langness Point (*Fl2, 30s, 21M*); Calf of Man (*Fl, 15s, 28M*); Chicken Rock (*Fl, 5s, 13M*); Port Erin, Raglan pierhead (*OcG, 5s, 5M*); Peel harbour breakwater head (*Oc, 7s, 6M*).

Cumbria coast:
Maryport S pierhead (*Fl, 1½s, 4M*); Workington S pierhead (*Fl, 5s, 8M*); Harrington pierhead (*FlG, 5s, 3M*); Whitehaven, N pierhead (*2FRvert, 9M*), W pierhead (*FlG, 5s, 13M*); St Bees Head (*Fl2, 20s, 21M*).

Morecambe Bay:
Walney (*Fl, 15s, 23M*); Lightning Knoll fairway buoy (*LFl, 10s*): Lune Deep buoy (*Q6+LFl, 15s*); Fleetwood leading lights in line 156°T—*front* (*FlY, 2s, 8M*), *rear* (*FlY, 4s, 11M*); River Lune leading lights in line 084°T—*front*, Plover Scar (*Fl, 2s, 11M*), *rear*, Cockersand Abbey (*F, 8M*); Glasson Quay (*FG, 1M*).

River Mersey approaches:
Bar LANBY (*Fl, 5s, 21M*); Queen's Channel 'Q1' light-float (*VQ*); Formby light-float (*Iso, 4s, 6M*); Crosby Channel 'C1' light buoy (*FlG, 3s*).

Anglesey and N entrance to Menai Strait:
Skerries (*Fl2, 10s, 22M; FR, 16M*); Point Lynas (*Oc, 10s, 20M*); Trwyn-Du (*Fl, 5½s, 15M*).

Irish coast;
Carlingford Lough entrance lighthouse (*Fl3, 10s, 20M*); Kilkeel pierhead (*Fl, WR, 2s, 8M*); Annalong E breakwater (*Oc, WRG, 5s, 9M*); St John's Point (*Q2, 7½s, 23M; FIWR, 3s, 15M, 11M*); Ardglass N pierhead (*Iso, WRG, 4s, 8M, 7M, 5M*); Strangford Lough, Angus Rock (*FIR, 5s, 6M*); South Rock light-ship (*Fl3R, 30s, 20M*); Portavogie (*Iso WRG, 5s, 9M*); Ballywalter (*Fl, WRG, 1½s,*

9M); Donaghadee S pierhead (*IsoWR, 4s, 18M, 14M*); Mew Island (*Fl4, 30s, 30M*); Black Head (*Fl, 3s, 27M*).

RDF Beacons

Walney Island light (*287.3, 'FN', 30M, Nos. 1, 4*); Point Lynas (*287.3, 'PS', 40M, Nos. 2, 5*); Douglas Victoria Pier (*287.3, 'DG', 50M, Nos. 3, 6*); Point of Ayre (*301.1, 'PY', 50M, No. 5*); Cregneish (*301.1, 'CN', 50M, No. 4*); Skerries (*301.1, 'SR', 50M, No. 1*); South Rock lightvessel (*301.1, 'SU', 50M, No. 6*); Ronaldsway aero beacon (*359, 'RWY', 20M, cont.*).

Weather Forecasts (all times GMT except where otherwise stated)

BBC shipping forecast area:
Irish Sea

VHF coast radio stations:
Anglesey—0833, 2033, on Ch. 26
Morecambe Bay—0803, 2003, on Ch. 04
Portpatrick—0833, 2033, on Ch. 27

Marinecall
Tel. 0898 500 460/461/465

Local radio coastal forecasts:
ILR Liverpool (Radio City)—Mon–Fri at 1315 local time; Sat/Sun at 0615, 0815. Frequencies: *1548 kHz, 194m, 96.7 MHz FM*; BBC Radio Lancashire—0735 and 0835 local time. Frequencies: *855/1557 kHz, 351/193m, 95.5/103.9/104.5 MHz FM*; BBC Radio Cumbria—Mon–Fri at local times 0715, 0815, 0840; Sat at 0830, 0935; Sun at 0830. Frequencies: *756/ 1458/837 kHz, 397/206/358m, 95.2/95.6/96.1/ 104.2 MHz FM*

Met Office forecasts:
An overall view can be obtained from Manchester Weather Centre, Tel. 061 477 1060

15 LARGS TO CARRICKFERGUS

The North Channel, in common with other constricted stretches of tidal water, has a rather capricious temperament. It may appear mild-mannered for much of the time, but it can turn irascible at short notice. At the narrowest part of the strait, between the Mull of Kintyre and Torr Head, Scotland and Northern Ireland are barely 11 miles apart. Farther S, it is more like 20 miles from the mouth of Belfast Lough across to Portpatrick harbour.

For strangers on passage, there is a curious sense of no-man's-land about this SE corner of sea area Malin. It feels no place to linger and most navigators are keen to get through and away whenever conditions look favourable. The tides run fairly hard in the North Channel, up to 4½ knots locally at springs to the SE of Rathlin Island and 2–2½ knots opposite Belfast Lough. A brisk north-westerly against the ebb kicks up a nasty brew, although a leading wind and a fair stream will make short work of your mileage.

The Channel forms a natural crossroads between some very different seascapes. A day sailing N can take you up to Islay or Jura and the start of the dramatic cruising of the Highlands and Islands. A day working S brings you round to the softer coast of Eire or maybe out to the Isle of Man. To the E are the outer reaches of the Firth of Clyde, while to the W you have the impressive cliff formations of County Antrim.

There are not many havens within easy reach of the North Channel, so you need to plan your passages with care if the weather is unsettled. Belfast Lough is the safest retreat on the Irish coast, with Carrickfergus Marina on its N side and Bangor harbour on the S. Lough Larne lies about 9 miles N along the coast from the entrance to Belfast Lough, not an especially attractive inlet but a secure anchorage none the less.

A few miles S of Belfast Lough, Donaghadee harbour is sheltered in westerlies and subject to swell in easterlies. Copelands Marina, just S of Donaghadee, is a peaceful half-tide basin formed from an old quarry. Portpatrick lies opposite Belfast Lough on the Galloway coast, a pier harbour whose narrow entrance can be unnerving to approach in fresh westerlies, dangerous in strong south-westerlies, but is quite snug once you are inside. The cross-tide off the entrance can reach 4½ knots. Eleven miles N of Portpatrick is Loch Ryan, a substantial inlet which has a reasonable anchorage on its W shore at The Wig.

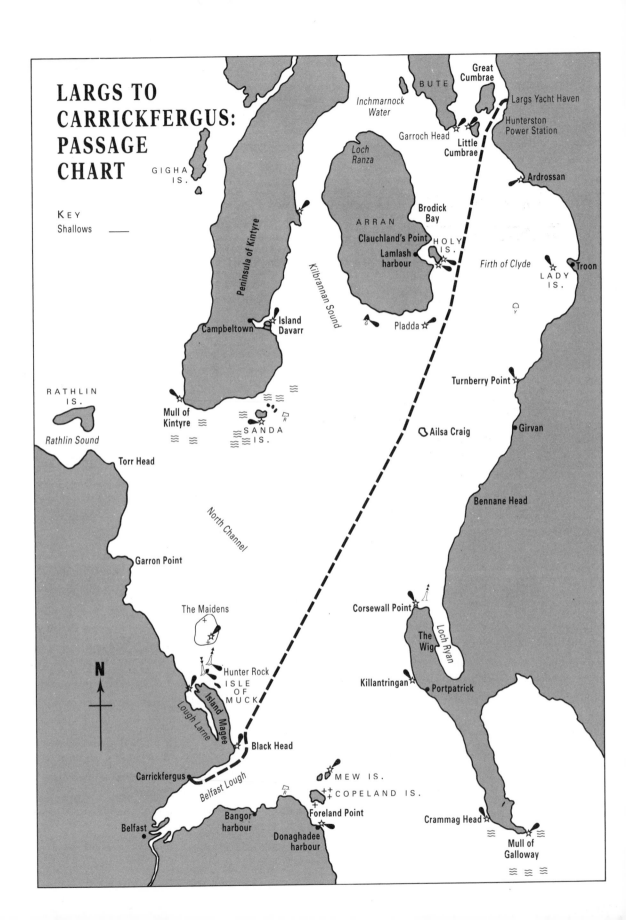

LARGS TO CARRICKFERGUS: PASSAGE CHART

GIGHA IS.

KEY
Shallows ———

Inchmarnock Water

BUTE

Great Cumbrae

Largs Yacht Haven

Garroch Head

Little Cumbrae

Hunterston Power Station

Loch Ranza

Ardrossan

Peninsula of Kintyre

ARRAN

Brodick Bay

Clauchland's Point

HOLY IS.

Lamlash harbour

Firth of Clyde

LADY IS.

Troon

Kilbrannan Sound

Campbeltown

Island Davarr

G

Pladda

Turnberry Point

RATHLIN IS.

Rathlin Sound

Mull of Kintyre

SANDA IS.

R

Ailsa Craig

Girvan

Torr Head

Bennane Head

North Channel

Garron Point

Corsewall Point

The Maidens

Loch Ryan

The Wig

N

Hunter Rock

ISLE OF MUCK

Killantringan

Portpatrick

Lough Larne

Island Magee

Black Head

Carrickfergus

Belfast Lough

MEW IS.

COPELAND IS.

R

Foreland Point

Crammag Head

Belfast

Bangor harbour

Donaghadee harbour

Mull of Galloway

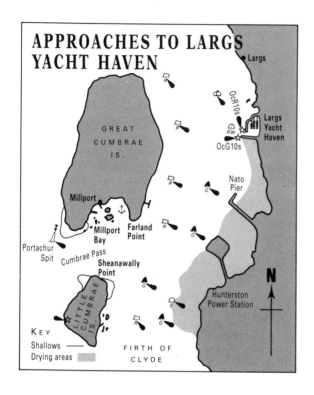

APPROACHES TO LARGS YACHT HAVEN

Largs

OcR10s

Largs
Yacht
Haven

OcG10s

GREAT
CUMBRAE
IS.

Nato
Pier

Millport

Millport   Farland
Bay   Point

Portachur
Spit   Cumbrae Pass

Sheanawally
Point

N

LITTLE
CUMBRAE
IS.

Hunterston
Power Station

KEY
Shallows ——
Drying areas

FIRTH OF
CLYDE

Campbeltown is a possible bolt-hole if you are caught out in the North Channel by strong westerlies or south-westerlies, a well-protected natural harbour on the SE corner of the Kintyre Peninsula. Coming from the S in heavy weather, you need to steer clear of the rocks and overfalls off Sanda Island, but you obtain increasing lee from the land as you draw N under Kintyre.

Although the most common weekend 'crossings' for local Irish yachts are from Belfast Lough to Portpatrick or Campbeltown, it is probably of wider interest to look at a longer passage between a Scottish and an Irish marina. Largs Yacht Haven lies well up the Firth of Clyde, tucked under the slopes of Blaeloch Hill and protected from the W by Great Cumbrae Island. As a cruising base, Largs has much to recommend it. There are protected waters close to hand, the Kyles of Bute are just a few hours'

sail away, yet the marina is near enough to the open sea that you can make a passage to Ireland in a long day if conditions are right.

It is approximately 75 miles from Largs to Carrickfergus, out past the low-lying Cumbraes and the forbidding heights of Arran, down the widening Firth to solitary Ailsa Craig and then across the North Channel into Belfast Lough. In reasonable visibility you have land in sight all the time, but it would be a grave mistake to think that you are sailing in nursery waters. The lower Firth of Clyde can feel extremely exposed in strong southerlies or south-westerlies, and the effects of hills and mountains can be quite complex in this part of the world. While you can reckon on smaller seas under the lee of land, you also find that high ground can significantly increase wind force locally, either by a funnelling effect if the wind is blowing along a narrow channel, or by downdraughts which are often experienced close under a mountainous weather shore. Arran is noted for both these effects.

A moderate north-westerly is a good wind for Largs to Carrickfergus, giving you a broad reach most of the way. The streams are weak in the Firth of Clyde, so the North Channel tides provide the main planning constraint. Other things being equal, and especially with a north-westerly, it is useful to be down off Ailsa Craig just before local LW, something like 6 hours after HW Dover. The stream would then have been trickling in your favour for much of the first part of the passage and be just starting to run S as you emerged from the Firth.

Ailsa Craig is almost a half-way mark, it being not quite 34 miles from Largs Yacht Haven to a waypoint 2 or 3 mile due W of Ailsa Craig, and then another 40 miles on to Carrickfergus. A period of neap tides has two advantages for this passage. The most important is that neap streams in the North Channel will not be too savage, which means that you will not be so vulnerable to steepening seas and overfalls if the weather should freshen.

The second advantage is that neap low tides come near the middle of the day hereabouts, so you could make an early morning start, be off Ailsa Craig about lunchtime, and aim to reach Carrickfergus in the evening. The benefits of neaps also apply to the return trip, although you can be more flexible about your departure coming back, depending on the wind and whether you'd prefer a fair or a predominantly slack tide in the North Channel.

If, for example, you were to leave Carrickfergus early in the morning, 1 hour or so before a neap high water, you would pick up the first of the ebb in the Channel and have more than enough northerly set to help you across to Ailsa Craig. However, it might be better to leave a bit earlier if the wind was a fresh north-westerly; you'd then be crossing open water either while the stream was still running S or it was just on the turn, hoping to have reached the outer part of the Firth of Clyde before the Channel became stirred up by the weather-going tide.

Leaving Largs

Setting off early from Largs is rarely a hardship. Even if the morning air is brisk and chilly, the sheltered sound between the mainland and Great Cumbrae provides easy sailing while you gradually come to life, get the coffee going and grill some bacon. Millport Bay opens up to starboard as you work down past Hunterston power station towards Little Cumbrae. You could, if you wished, take the pass between Great and Little Cumbrae, a scenic diversion which will only add on a mile or two.

Once clear of Little Cumbrae, the general heading is S and a bit W for a position 3–4 miles E of Pladda, a small skerry off the SE tip of Arran. In north-westerlies or westerlies, don't come too close

to Arran on this leg or you will be plagued by fluky shifts in the lee of Goat Fell and Tighvein.

Off Pladda, and given a leading wind, you can either lay off a single course to take you across to Black Head and the entrance to Belfast Lough, or you can make for an intermediate waypoint first, perhaps a position a couple of miles W of Ailsa Craig. The latter is often a better bet, because you don't really pick up much tide until you get out into the mouth of the Firth.

Crossing the North Channel

It is about 34 miles from the Ailsa Craig waypoint to a position 1 mile SE of Black Head, probably 5 to 6 hours' sailing with a fair wind and the tide helping you S. When allowing for the flood, better to overestimate the stream than to underestimate, holding up to the N of Belfast Lough until you are comfortably within reach of Black Head. In fresh weather at springs, you can meet some locally steep seas in the vicinity of the Mermaid Shoal, which lies 11½ miles SW of Ailsa Craig.

As you get over towards the Irish coast, you can take a useful set of bearings off East Maiden lighthouse, the tall radio mast on Island Magee and Black Head lighthouse. Fixes from these three can give you a good idea of your south-easterly set as you approach Belfast Lough. Keep an eye open for the Stranraer to Larne ferries out in the North Channel, especially if visibility is poor, and watch out for other shipping which might be converging on Belfast Lough.

From Black Head to Carrickfergus is just over 5 miles and it is best to keep 1 mile offshore to clear Cloghan and Kilroot jetties, Kilroot power station intake basin, and the wide shoal area in the bay W of Kilroot Point. The power-station chimney is a very prominent mark, nearly 200 m high. Carrickfergus harbour lies about 1½ miles WSW of the chimney and Carrickfergus Castle is conspicuous right at the root of the E breakwater. The marina occupies a comparatively new artificial basin, not quite 2 cables W of the main harbour entrance, and entry is straightforward by day or night at practically any state of tide. The visitors' berths are to port as you come in. Carrickfergus Marina is dredged to 1.8 m and has all the usual facilities.

Poor Visibility

Belfast Lough can be tricky to approach in murky visibility, because the only useful RDF beacon is Mew Island, on the S side of the entrance (*294.2kHz, 'MW', 50M, No. 2*). If conditions are very thick, you can aim to make your landfall on Island Magee, midway between the Isle of Muck and Black Head. This stretch of coast is steep-to, so there is no great danger in edging close inshore. The soundings are not very helpful, but a bearing of Mew Island beacon, only about 9 miles away, should give an accurate idea of your distance off. If you are reasonably confident of your position when you sight land, you can turn sharp left and feel your way along the coast to Black Head.

Heavy Weather on Passage

If, on passage from Largs to Carrickfergus, you are assailed by heavy weather from a southerly quarter, you always have the option of running back to Largs. With any W in the wind, Lamlash can be a useful refuge, behind Holy Island on the E side of Arran. The narrow S entrance to this natural harbour leads between Fullarton Rock red buoy (*Fl2R, 12s*) and Holy Island SW light (*FlG, 3s*). There are some moorings and an anchorage ½ mile to port as you come through this channel, but most yachts fetch up off Lamlash town in westerlies. Watch out for the large unlit Admiralty buoys on the way over to the town anchorage.

The N entrance to Lamlash is wider than the S, and yachts can pass Hamilton Spit red buoy either side, so long as Hamilton Rock is left at least 200 m to starboard as you come in past Clauchland's Point. In strong easterlies you can anchor off the NW shore of Holy Island, just opposite a solitary farmhouse.

From a point a couple of miles W of Ailsa Craig, Lamlash and Campbeltown are both 17 miles distant. Campbeltown, a small loch on the SE side of Kintyre, is more secure than Lamlash, but may be harder to reach from the outer Firth if there is too much W in the wind. When approaching Campbeltown in heavy weather, careful navigation is needed so that you pass just N of Island Davarr (*Fl2, 10s*) and line up nicely for the entrance.

Troon harbour, with its sheltered inner marina, lies on the mainland side of the Firth of Clyde immediately opposite Holy Island. Because of its location well to the E, you would probably only consider Troon on a passage from Largs to Carrickfergus if a north-westerly with which you started turned out to be stronger than you anticipated once you drew away from Little Cumbrae.

In strong south-easterlies, Girvan is worth bearing in mind if you can work up to it, a small harbour on the Ayrshire coast just over 8 miles E of Ailsa Craig. Enter above half-tide from the WNW, keeping the S pier close to starboard.

Loch Ryan is a useful refuge in heavy westerly weather and the attractive anchorage at The Wig offers good protection from this quarter. The Clyde Cruising Club directions note that, in NW gales, particularly steep seas can build up just outside the entrance to Loch Ryan, especially during the N-going stream. Farther down the coast, Portpatrick

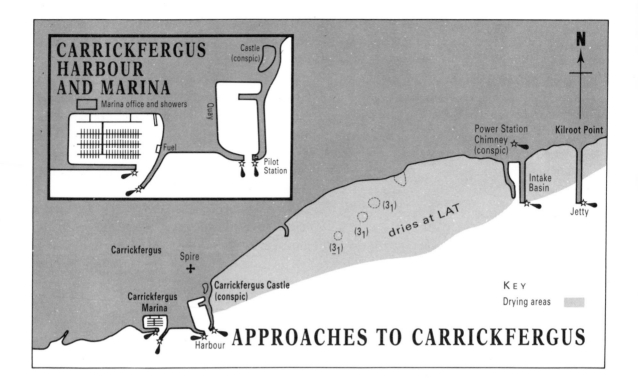

CARRICKFERGUS HARBOUR AND MARINA

Marina office and showers

Quay

Fuel

Castle (conspic)

Pilot Station

Power Station Chimney (conspic)

Kilroot Point

Intake Basin

Jetty

(3_1)

(3_1)

(3_1)

$(\underline{3}_1)$

dries at LAT

Carrickfergus

Spire

Carrickfergus Castle (conspic)

Carrickfergus Marina

Harbour

APPROACHES TO CARRICKFERGUS

K E Y

Drying areas

is no place to run to in any strong winds from the W, although it is secure and safe to enter in easterlies. On the passage from Largs to Carrickfergus, Portpatrick may be a welcome bolt-hole if you are overtaken by heavy north-easterly weather, and prefer to tuck under the lee of Galloway rather than run on across the North Channel.

Over on the Irish side, Lough Larne is worth keeping in mind if, for example, a favourable easterly with which you started the passage shifts into the SE and freshens. You can get into Larne at any state of tide, by day or night, but it is important to give a wide berth to The Maidens and Hunter Rock in the outer approaches, where the tides run strongly.

Belfast Lough is straightforward to enter, especially on its N side. On the S side you have to avoid the various rocky shoals between Mew Island and Copeland Island, and between Copeland and Foreland Point. A weather-going tide or a fresh onshore wind kicks up heavy overfalls to the E of Mew Island.

Carrickfergus Marina is secure and safe to enter in almost any weather, although it is hard work beating up Belfast Lough in a strong south-westerly. On the opposite side of the Lough, Bangor is well protected in winds with any S in them, and it can sometimes be preferable to work up towards this weather shore rather than claw along a lee shore between Black Head and Carrickfergus.

High-speed Factors

An increasing number of power boats are based in the Firth of Clyde, either at Largs Yacht Haven or at one of the other marinas, Kip or Troon. The upper part of the Firth is well sheltered, but the lower reaches between Arran and the mainland can serve up some hard conditions at relatively short notice. The surrounding mountains cause local and fast-changing weather variations, so that fast motor boats can sometimes benefit from being able to take advantage of quiet spells for passage-making. By the same token, though, you must never assume that a calm patch is going to last for very long. Always aim to reach your destination as quickly as possible, and have one or two bolt-holes worked out in case you can't quite make it.

The 74-mile passage from Largs Yacht Haven to Carrickfergus Marina will take 5 hours at 15 knots and 3¾ hours if you can average 20 knots. Your most vulnerable part of the passage is the ill-reputed North Channel, where even a moderate wind against the tide will kick up steep seas that can quickly force you off the plane. Your strategy should centre around dead slack water in the North Channel, which is either ½ hour before or 5½ hours after HW Dover. The departure time from Largs or Carrickfergus should therefore be worked out so that you arrive in the middle of the North Channel at one of these slack periods. From Largs you can reckon on something like 50 miles to reach mid-Channel, and from Carrickfergus about 20 miles.

The high ground in this area provides plenty of good radar targets, but the only Racon beacon is on Sanda Island ('T', 20M) off the Mull of Kintyre. In poor visibility, Ailsa Craig is an important target out in the mouth of the Firth of Clyde.

Pilot Books, etc.

Clyde Cruising Club Directions, *Firth of Clyde*.

Irish Cruising Club Sailing Directions, *East and North Coasts of Ireland*.

Admiralty NP66, *West Coast of Scotland Pilot*.

Admiralty NP40, *Irish Coast Pilot*.

Admiralty NP74, *List of Lights, Vol. A*.

Note: The Clyde Cruising Club and Irish Cruising Club directions can be obtained by post from Clyde Cruising Club Publications, S.V. 'Carrick', Clyde Street, Glasgow G1 4LN, Tel. 041 552 2183.

Admiralty Charts

No. 2724—North Channel to the Firth of Lorne

No. 1907—Little Cumbrae Island to Cloch Point

No. 1864—Harbours and anchorages in the Firth of Clyde

No. 2198—North Channel, southern part

No. 2199—North Channel, northern part

No. 1753—Belfast Lough

Tidal Atlases

Admiralty NP218, *North coast of Ireland and West coast of Scotland*.

Tidal Streams (times based on HW Dover)

Position	N-going stream starts	S-going stream starts
Firth of Clyde 5 miles SE of Pladda	−0500	+0140
10 miles SW of Ailsa Craig	+0030	−0600
North Channel off Island Magee	−0015	+0545

Tidal Differences and Heights

Place	Time of HW on Dover	Heights above chart datum in metres			
		MHWS	MLWS	MHWN	MLWN
Largs	+0100	3.4	0.5	2.8	1.0
Lamlash	+0050	3.2	0.4	2.7	1.0
Campbeltown	+0045	3.0	0.4	2.5	0.9
Girvan	+0045	3.1	0.4	2.6	0.9
Portpatrick	+0035	3.8	0.3	3.0	0.9
Larne	+0010	2.8	0.4	2.5	0.8
Carrickfergus	+0005	3.5	0.4	3.0	1.1

Important Lights

Firth of Clyde:

Largs Yacht Haven—W breakwater head (*OcR, 10s*), S breakwater head (*OcG, 10s*); Little Cumbrae Elbow (*Fl, 3s, 23M, vis 334°-210°T*); Rubhan Eun, SE tip Isle of Bute (*FlR, 6s, 12M*); Holy Island main light (*Fl2, 20s, 25M*); Holy Island SW light (*FlG, 3s, 10M, vis 282°-147°T*); Pladda (*Fl3, 30s, 23M*); Lady Island (*Fl4, 30s, 8M*); Troon W pierhead—main light (*OcWR, 6s, 5M, R vis 036°-090°T, W vis 090°-036°T*), SE light on dolphin (*FlWG, 3s, 5M, G vis 146°-318°T, W vis 318°-146°T*); Troon E pierhead (*2FRvert, 5M, obscured bearing more than 199°T*); Turnberry Point (*Fl, 15s, 24M*); Ailsa Craig (*Fl6, 30s, 17M, vis 145°-028°T*).

Kintyre Peninsula:

Island Davarr (*Fl2, 10s, 23M*); Campbeltown leading lights (*2 fixed orange lights in line bearing 240°T*); Sanda Island (*FlWR, 24s, W19M vis 267°T-shore, R16M vis 245°-267°T*); Mull of Kintyre (*Fl2, 20s, 29M, vis 347°-178°T*).

North Channel, E side:

Corsewall Point (*AltWR, 74s, 18M, vis 027°-257°T*); Killantringan, Black Head (*Fl2, 15s, 25M*); Portpatrick leading lights (*2FG in line bearing 050°T*); Crammag Head (*Fl, 10s, 18M*); Mull of Galloway (*Fl, 20s, 28M, vis 182°-105°T*).

North Channel, W side:

East Maiden (*Fl3, 20s, 23M; Aux Lt FlR, 5s, 8M, vis 142°-182°T*); Larne entrance, Chaine Tower (*IsoWR, 5s, 11M, W vis 230°-240°T, R vis 240°T-shore*); Larne entrance, Ferris Point (*Iso WRG, 10s, 17M, 13M, 13M, vis W 345°-119°T, G 119°-154°T, W 154°-201°T, R 201°-223°T*); Larne leading lights in line 184°T (*2 sync Oc4s, 12M, vis 179°-189°T*); Island Magee, Black Head (*Fl, 3s, 27M*); Cloghan Jetty—N end (*FlG, 3s*), S end (*FlG, 3s*); Kilroot Point Jetty (*OcG, 10s*); Kilroot intake digue (*OcG 4s*); Kilroot power station chimney (*2QR*); Carrickfergus harbour—E pierhead (*FlG, 7.5s, 2M, vis 050°-255°T*), W pierhead (*FlR, 7.5s, 2M, vis 068°-256°T*); Carrickfergus Marina—E breakwater head (*QG, 3M*), W breakwater head (*QR, 3M, obscured 245°-305°T*); Mew Island (*Fl4, 30s, 30M*); Donaghadee S pierhead (*IsoWR, 4s, W18M vis shore-326°T, R14M vis 326°-shore*).

RDF Beacons

Pladda (*294.2kHz, 'DA', 30M, No. 1*); Mew Island (*294.2kHz, 'MW', 50M, No. 2*); Altacarry Head, Rathlin Island (*294.2kHz, 'AH', 50M, No. 3*); Turnberry aero beacon (*355kHz, 'TRN', 50M, cont.*); Belfast aero beacon (*275kHz, 'HB', 15M, cont.*) has a low range and is susceptible to land effects.

Local Information

For any further information about Largs or Carrickfergus, contact either:

Carolyn Elder, Largs Yacht Haven, Irvine Road, Largs, Ayrshire KA30 8EZ, Tel. 0475 675333

John McCormick, Carrickfergus Marina, Rodgers Quay, Carrickfergus, County Antrim BT38 8BU, Tel. 09603 66666.

Weather Forecasts (all times GMT except where otherwise stated)

BBC shipping forecast area:
  Malin

VHF coast radio stations:
  Clyde—0833, 2033, on Ch. 26
  Portpatrick—0833, 2033, on Ch. 27

Marinecall:
  Tel. 0898 500 462

Local radio coastal forecasts:
  ILR Glasgow (Radio Clyde)—at local times 0605, 0705, 0805, 0915, 1630; frequencies: *1152 kHz, 261m, 102.5 MHz FM*. ILR Belfast (Downtown Radio)—coastal forecasts/warnings given on the hour or half-hour when available; frequencies: *1029 kHz, 292m, 96.4/96.6/97.4/102.4 MHz FM*

Met Office forecasts:
  Glasgow Weather Centre, Tel. 041 248 3451
  Belfast (Aldergrove) Airport, Tel. 084 94 52339

16 HIGH-SPEED NAVIGATION

When comparative newcomers to motor boating start making offshore passages, they are soon aware of a definite gap between navigation theory (carefully studied, perhaps, during the winter) and what is actually possible in practice. This gap tends to be most pronounced for fast-planing boats, where the crew quickly discover the difficulties involved in working over a chart table at 20 knots in a bit of a chop.

It also becomes obvious that, at this sort of speed, a navigator is pressed for time. In the ten minutes it might take to work out a new course, you will travel more than 3 miles, possibly into dangerous water. This is a far cry from navigating a displacement boat at a leisurely 6 or 7 knots, where it is relatively easy on passage to peruse the chart, mark up your estimated position every hour, or plot a set of bearings as soon as you have taken them.

When cruising at high speed, it makes sense to do as much of the navigation as possible before you set out. It is useful to draw an analogy with flying, where the pilot works out a precise flight-plan before taking off. This plan will consist of a series of legs between convenient waypoints, with wind drift taken into account for an aircraft in the same way as a yacht navigator allows for tidal streams. Each leg is specified in terms of course to steer, distance, and elapsed time at a given speed.

Although the widespread use of Decca has indirectly promoted the flight-plan idea among yachtsmen, it is a practical system for any high-speed boat, even if there are no electronic aids aboard at all. Modern sportsboats, for instance, are capable of fast coastal passages in moderate weather, and yet their navigation facilities are apt to be somewhat limited. For a weekend cruise, you could work out a number of possible plans in advance at home and thus be well prepared for passage-making when you arrive at your boat on a Friday evening or Saturday morning.

The 'Flight-plan'

It is a good idea to use some kind of pro forma for setting out your passage plan. The example in Figure 1 was designed by Cameron Meikle of Jersey, but you could easily devise something similar to suit your own way of working. At the head of each sheet are entered the height and time of high water at the reference port for tidal stream information. Then comes the departure time, which I normally take as the expected time at the first waypoint; you

Date: _____   From: _____   To: _____

Height of tide: _____   Time high water: _____   Depart: HW _____

Local mag. variation: _____   Cruising speed: _____   Log readings: Finish:
                                                                                Start: _____

From	WP	To	WP	Track °True	Tidal stream knots.	Tidal stream °True	Course °True	Course °Mag	Dev	Steer °Mag	Dist NM	SMG knots	Time	E.T.A.	A.T.A.

Reproduced by courtesy of *Motor Boat and Yachting*

Figure 1 A planning sheet designed for high-speed passage-making (copyright Cameron Meikle)

can either express this in the 24-hour clock, or as a difference before or after HW. There are also spaces for local magnetic variation, likely cruising speed and the initial log reading.

The main part of the form is for the navigational details of each leg of the passage. You will notice that there are columns for waypoint reference numbers, which makes it easy for you to enter a Decca 'sail-plan' to match your flight-plan. The data columns are filled in as follows:

Track: The direct course between waypoints, in degrees true.

Tidal stream: An estimated average rate (in knots) and direction of flow (in degrees true) over the expected duration of the leg.

Course (true): The calculated course to compensate for the tide, in degrees true.

Course (mag.): The previous column expressed in degrees magnetic, that is, after applying variation.

Deviation: The magnetic deviation for that particular heading, obtained from the ship's deviation card.

Steer: The final course, corrected for ship's deviation, that is, the course that you actually steer by compass.

Distance: The leg distance, measured directly between waypoints in nautical miles.

Speed made good: The effective speed 'over the ground' between waypoints, obtained from the length of the track side of the tidal triangle when you worked out the course to steer.

Time: The calculated time to cover the leg.

ETA: The estimated time of arrival at the next waypoint.

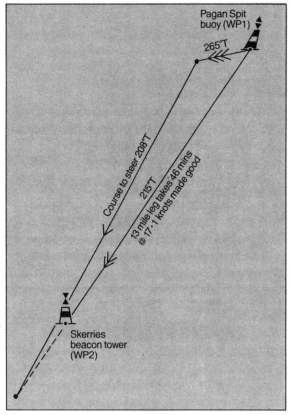

Pagan Spit
buoy (WP1)

265°T

Course to steer 208°T

215°T

13 mile leg takes 46 mins
@ 17·1 knots made good

Skerries
beacon tower
(WP2)

Reproduced by courtesy of *Motor Boat and Yachting*

Figure 2 Calculating the course to steer for the first leg of the passage shown in Figure 3

ATA: The actual time of arrival at that waypoint, with the log reading at that time alongside it.

You can see that completing the plan involves basic chartwork to allow for the effect of tidal streams and to work out the course to steer for each leg (see Figure 2). The layout of the form encourages the navigator to be systematic about this, but it also highlights the importance of calculating accurate leg distances and times when you are travelling at fast cruising speeds. If one of your waypoints is an offshore buoy, for example, and it hasn't turned up at its ETA, you know that something is wrong somewhere. At slow cruising speeds, you might not be

too concerned if a buoy was even 15 minutes late in appearing; at 20 knots, though, 15 minutes represents 5 miles, which is a considerable error if you haven't spotted the mark you were trying to find.

On high-speed passages I use a small digital count-down timer (bought cheaply as a kitchen timer) which can quickly be reset at the start of each leg. Counting down to the next beacon is standard practice in aviation, to continue the flight-plan analogy, but the sense is also consistent with a Decca display of distance to next waypoint, or a radar range reading. So if you have full instrumentation, the count-down routine makes it easy to double check your progress, especially if you keep a calculator handy in the wheelhouse—3 miles to go by Decca or radar should mean 9 minutes left on the clock at 20 knots made good.

Contingency Planning

Of course a 'flight-plan' is very reassuring in high-speed navigation if everything goes as it should, but you obviously need to make some kind of provision for changes of plan. Deteriorating weather—freshening winds, say, or poor visibility—would probably give you plenty to worry about without the problem of having to calculate a series of new legs at short notice. The prudent skipper will look ahead and try to specify some alternative routes *before* putting to sea. For example, the passage from Port Pagan to Ferrymouth shown in Figure 3 has three natural legs:

1 From Pagan Spit E-cardinal buoy to the Skerries beacon tower.
2 From the Skerries to West Gun LANBY.
3 From West Gun LANBY to Ferrymouth fairway buoy.

There are, however, two other possible destinations

that you may need to consider: Port Grimm and Quick Head. Port Grimm could be a useful bolt-hole if visibility clamped in and you felt that it would be a bit risky to try and locate the West Gun LANBY. Quick Head might be handy if the weather were to pick up from the N and make Ferrymouth bar a risky choice. You could therefore introduce two notional 'decision' waypoints into your passage—X being midway between the Skerries and West Gun LANBY, and Y midway between West Gun LANBY and Ferrymouth fairway buoy.

This would give you six passage waypoints, including the Pagan Spit departure point. If you planned to cast off from Port Pagan just before 0900, you might reckon on 0930 at Pagan Spit buoy. Your cruising speed should be 16 knots if the sea is quiet. The tide will be more or less W-going until 1100, slack for ½ hour or so, and then E-going from 1130.

Your main 'flight-plan' will look something like Figure 4, the tidal information having been extracted from the relevant tidal atlas. I would treat the Skerries to West Gun Bank as one leg, taking waypoint X to be half-way along either by the log or the clock. Similarly, West Gun to Ferrymouth fairway could be calculated as one leg, with waypoint Y being reached after half the leg distance had been run or half the leg time had elapsed.

Your ETA at Ferrymouth fairway buoy is 1215, so if all goes well you should be entering the river a couple of hours before HW, with a respectable depth over the bar. But having worked out this plan, you can now calculate two useful contingency legs—waypoint X to a position ½ mile due S of Bass Point and waypoint Y to a position ¾ mile N of Quick Head. You can take the departure times from X and Y to be the respective ETAs in the main plan—the tide flows broadly E or W, so it won't make much difference to the courses if you arrive at X or Y a little early or late.

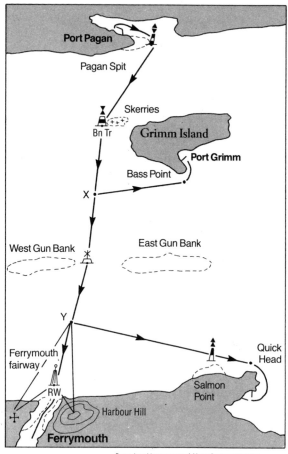

Reproduced by courtesy of *Motor Boat and Yachting*

Figure 3 The passage from Pagan to Ferrymouth, complete with contingency plans

There are now eight possible waypoints, as follows:

1—Pagan Spit E-cardinal buoy.
2—Skerries beacon tower.
3—Contingency waypoint X.
4—West Gun LANBY.
5—Contingency waypoint Y.
6—Ferrymouth fairway buoy.
7—Bass Point (½ mile S).
8—Quick Head (¾ mile N).

If you have Decca, these waypoints should be care-

Date: 11th March 89   From: Port Pagan   To: Ferrymouth

Height of tide: 4·1m   Time high water: 1433 (Ferrymouth) Depart: HW −5hrs (0930)

Local mag. variation: 5°W   Cruising speed: 16kts   Log readings: Finish:
                                                  Start: _____

From	WP	To	WP	Track °True	Tidal stream knots	Tidal stream °True	Course °True	Course °Mag	Dev	Steer °Mag	Dist NM	SMG knots	Time	E.T.A.	A.T.A.
Pagan Spit	1	Skerries	2	215	2	265	208	213	3°E	210	13·0	14·1	46min	1016	
Skerries	2	W/P X	3	190	1½	255	186	191	1°E	190				1044	
W/P X	3	West Gun	4	190	1	255	186	191	1°E	190	14·5	16·4	56min	1112	
West Gun	4	W/P Y	5	194	SLACK		199	204	2°E	202				1143	
W/P Y	5	Ferrymouth Fairway	6	194	1	085	199	204	2°E	202	16·5	15·8	63min	1215	
W/P X	3	Bass Point	7	084	SLACK		084	089	2°W	091	12·0	16	45min		
W/P Y	5	Quick Head	8	103	1½	085	105	110	2°W	112	25·0	17·4	86min		

Reproduced by courtesy of *Motor Boat and Yachting*

Figure 4 The completed planning sheet. The layout of the form encourages the navigator to be systematic

fully entered and checked before you set off, with the sail-plan specified as route 1–2–3–4–5–6. If you wanted to be really thorough, you could work out two further contingency legs for the flight-plan: West Gun LANBY to Bass Point (4–7) and West Gun LANBY to Quick Head (4–8). You are now well prepared for the passage to Ferrymouth, with various changes of plan ready if you need them. Try to arrive at Pagan Spit buoy as close to 0930 as possible, set your count-down timer to 46 minutes for the first leg, come on to 210° compass, open the throttles and away you go.

Landfall Planning

The transition between the open sea and the coast is critical and sometimes rather traumatic. At sea,

given reasonable weather and a well-found boat, you are relatively safe—even if you're not sure exactly where you are! It is when you close the shore that potential dangers start to raise their heads. Stronger tides, steeper seas, rocks, shoals and sandbanks are usually features of landfalls, not of passage-making. For this reason it is a mistake to heave a sigh of relief when you sight the coast. Your problems, far from being over, are usually just beginning.

When compiling a flight-plan, don't stop as soon as you have calculated an ETA at one of the outer buoys (i.e. Ferrymouth fairway in the above example). There are two further pieces of preparation: the first is to devise some landfall checks, and the second is to trace the final route into harbour. Landfall checks are particularly important when

PILOTAGE SHEET No. 6 :- Approaches to Ferrymouth				
Name of mark	Description	Left to:	By:	Approx distance to next mark
Ferrymouth fairway	RW with Sph topmark	Starboard	Close	1½ M @ 185°C
Ferrymouth No 1	Green conic	Starboard	50m	200m SSW
Ferrymouth No 2	Red can	Port	50m	¼ M
Ferrymouth No 3	Green conic	Starboard	Close	¼ M
King's Flat beacon	Green Spar	Starboard	25m	½ M due S
Viper's Bank beacon	W-cardinal	Port	50m	—
Thereafter to anchorage on port hand, outside the moorings and just opposite the second jetty.				

Figure 5 The final part of a flight plan passage – a list of buoys and beacons at the harbour entrance

you are cruising at high speed. At 6 knots in a displacement boat, you have time to study the emerging coast through the glasses, compare what you see with the large-scale chart, and gradually identify features as you draw inshore. There is more urgency at 16 knots and it is advisable to have worked out one or two clear transits or bearings that can indicate whether or not you are approaching on the right track.

Figure 3 shows the contours of a hill on the E side of Ferrymouth estuary, the summit of which ought to be bearing due S true from waypoint Y, 12 miles distant and easily identified in good visibility; as you approach the fairway buoy this bearing will decrease to about 150°T. There is also a church spire on the W side of the entrance, which should bear 215°T from Y, increasing to 235°T as you near the buoy.

It is worth knowing in advance what these bearing sectors should be, because they can provide you with some quick navigational reassurance even as you sit at the wheel. This all helps to complete the partial picture provided by your other sources of information; the leg timer will be counting down towards zero, the Decca 'distance to next waypoint' will be steadily decreasing and the 'bearing to next waypoint' should be more or less steady, but increasing very slightly as the first of the E-going tide brings you back on to track.

When you finally pick up the fairway buoy visually and provided it seems to be in more or less the right place, you should head right up towards it, in order to make a *positive identification* before starting the final run in. You can now refer to the last part of your flight-plan—a list of entrance buoys and beacons, in the order in which they should appear. Figure 5 gives an example for the near approaches to Ferrymouth.

The faster your cruising speed, the more important it is to prepare you flight-plan carefully. I began by emphasizing the physical difficulties of navigating at high speed, as well as the sheer pressure of time. But there is also a psychological factor; at high speeds, the sense of uncertainty, if you lose track of your position, is somehow compounded. At 20 knots, you are not merely approaching some real or imagined danger, you seem to be hurtling headlong towards it. The flight-plan helps avoid this uncomfortable sensation, by at least creating the impression that you are more or less in control of your passage-making.

Sea Areas Maps

Right: British sea areas as used in shipping forecasts plus the numbers of common areas used by countries surrounding the North Sea including France *(courtesy Alan Watts)*

Below: French sea areas excluding the common ones in the North Sea

(courtesy Alan Watts)

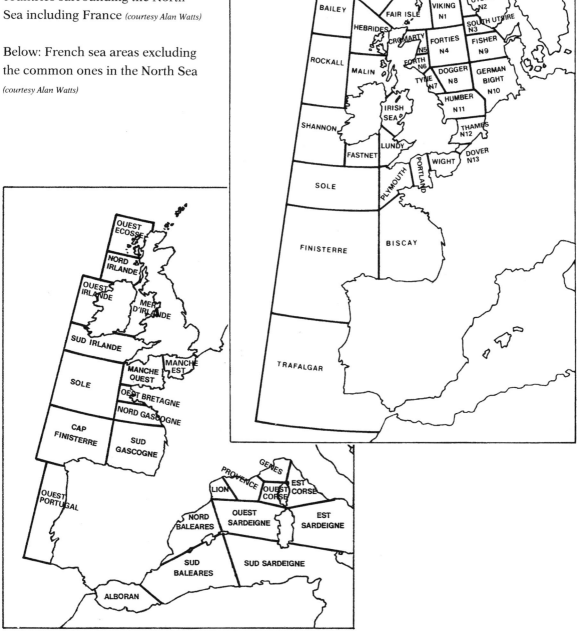

INDEX